Includes 100 Recipes *for Easy Weeknight* **Dinners, Better Boxed Lunches, Healthier Desserts,** *and More!*

The Anti-Inflammatory Family Cookbook

The Kid-Friendly, Pediatrician-Approved Way to *Transform Your Family's Health*

Stefania Patinella, Alexandra Romey,
Hilary McClafferty, MD, FAAP,
Jonathan Deutsch, PhD, and
Maria Mascarenhas, MBBS

Adams Media
New York   London   Toronto   Sydney   New Delhi

A adams media

Adams Media
An Imprint of Simon & Schuster, Inc.
57 Littlefield Street
Avon, Massachusetts 02322

First Adams Media trade paperback edition January 2021

ADAMS MEDIA and colophon are trademarks of Simon & Schuster.

For information about special discounts for bulk purchases, please contact Simon & Schuster Special Sales at 1-866-506-1949 or business@simonandschuster.com.

The Simon & Schuster Speakers Bureau can bring authors to your live event. For more information or to book an event contact the Simon & Schuster Speakers Bureau at 1-866-248-3049 or visit our website at www.simonspeakers.com.

Interior design by Erin Alexander
Interior layout by Katrina Machado
Photographs by Harper Point Photography
Pediatric Anti-Inflammatory Food Table (page 37) copyright © Hilary McClafferty

Manufactured in the United States of America

10 9 8 7 6 5 4 3 2 1

Library of Congress Cataloging-in-Publication Data has been applied for.

ISBN 978-1-5072-1297-4
ISBN 978-1-5072-1298-1 (ebook)

Contents

Introduction

Berries, broccoli, avocados—these are just some of the many anti-inflammatory foods that promote better health, ward off diseases, and lead to a longer and healthier life. These inflammation-fighting foods are tasty, nutritious, offer whole body benefits, and are great for children (and grownups too!). By learning which foods calm or prevent inflammation in the body, you'll be able to create meals and snacks for your loved ones that can not only satisfy their taste buds but boost their health as well.

The Anti-Inflammatory Family Cookbook is here to help by explaining the important, science-based health benefits of feeding your family anti-inflammatory foods *and* giving you easy, practical ways to make anti-inflammatory eating enjoyable for everyone. You can think of us as your personal guides, chefs, and pediatricians. As chefs, we'll help you adapt recipes and guide you in the kitchen with more than one hundred recipes for foods like Breakfast Tostadas, Vegetable Pita Pizzas, Fish Tacos, Creamy Chicken Soup, and Dark Chocolate Bark. As pediatricians, we'll explain the most up-to-date science in an easily digestible way so you can make informed choices.

More than just a series of food rules, this book centers on the enjoyment of delicious, whole foods as a foundation of better health. Inside you'll find information on the following:

- What inflammation is and why it matters
- The core tenets of anti-inflammatory eating
- Advice on how to be a smart food shopper, including how to make sense of nutrition labels and avoid additives
- Strategies for expanding your children's palates so they genuinely enjoy anti-inflammatory foods

- How to make mealtimes happy and relaxed, and avoid food battles
- How to make substitutions, accommodate food allergies, and prep ahead to make mealtimes easier
- One hundred recipes for all types of food—from anti-inflammatory spice blends to easy dinners, nutritious snacks, and delicious and healthy desserts

You will also find step-by-step instructions for getting your kids involved in cooking, which is one of the best strategies for encouraging healthy eating! With *The Anti-Inflammatory Family Cookbook*, you'll have the knowledge and recipes you need to get your family healthier while keeping them happy too!

CHAPTER 1

The Anti-Inflammatory Way and Why It Is Important for Children

This introductory chapter will lay the foundation for the anti-inflammatory way and answer some important questions: What is inflammation? Why does it matter? And what does food have to do with inflammation? You'll learn the history of the anti-inflammatory diet and the core tenets of the anti-inflammatory way, including which foods are most beneficial and which to avoid. Finally, this chapter will define and demystify some concepts you may have heard and wondered about, like flavonoids, antioxidants, whole grains, artificial sweeteners, additives, and more.

WHAT IS INFLAMMATION?

Although this book is about the anti-inflammatory diet, it's important to explain that not all inflammation is bad! In fact, inflammation is part of the body's healing mechanisms and immune response. For example, if your child scrapes her knee, her body will immediately respond with an inflammatory process. Around her knee will be the characteristic four signs of inflammation—redness, swelling, pain, and heat. Underneath the skin, her body is initiating a cascade of events that will help her heal the wound. While a scraped knee hurts, it's amazing how quickly it can heal—this is a sign of the body's resilience and health. This kind of short-term inflammation is fast and fiery. It comes to the rescue when needed, helps resolve the injury, and cools down until the next time it is needed.

Chronic inflammation is different. It is not a response to a specific wound, but to many stressors in the body, such as lack of sleep, environmental pollutants, unhealthy foods, infections, overwork, and trauma of all kinds. It also includes those feelings of overwhelm or anxiety that we ordinarily think of as "stress," which is present in abundance in the modern world. When the body experiences an excess of any of these stressors (or often a combination of them), chronic inflammation can set in, which in turn profoundly impacts health. Imagine the intense, localized inflammation on that scraped knee spreading throughout the whole body. But because it's internal, we usually aren't aware of it in the same way as a scraped knee will continually draw our attention until it is healed. It slowly and steadily inflicts damage. Today we know that chronic inflammation is associated with a long list of diseases, including obesity, diabetes, asthma, inflammatory bowel disease, high blood pressure, high cholesterol, arthritis, and cancers, among other conditions. New science even shows how chronic inflammation and the microbiome are closely linked to mental health conditions like depression, anxiety, attention deficit hyperactivity disorder (ADHD), and Alzheimer's. While we think of most of those as adult diseases, many are occurring much more frequently in children and adolescents. Fortunately, many of these conditions are also preventable.

WHAT IS THE ANTI-INFLAMMATORY WAY?

The anti-inflammatory way is not exactly a "diet"—at least not in the sense that conjures food deprivation. More than a series of food rules, the anti-inflammatory way reflects a lifestyle modeled on traditional cultures where the enjoyment of delicious, whole foods is a foundation of family life. At dinner tables around the world, good taste and good health are not at odds with each other. This is one of the core tenets of the anti-inflammatory way: Nourishment and pleasure go hand in hand.

The term "anti-inflammatory" in relation to diet was adopted by Dr. Andrew Weil in the late 1990s. The approach was modeled after two diets, the Mediterranean diet and the Okinawa or Japanese diet, which are two cultural eating patterns that have been shown in countless studies to be especially health protective. Studies show that in both adults and children, eating a daily diet of anti-inflammatory foods measurably decreases inflammatory markers and many of the conditions associated with inflammation. Consider the following examples:

- In adults, the anti-inflammatory diet has been linked to decreased illness and mortality from numerous chronic diseases, including cardiovascular diseases, diabetes, invasive breast cancer and other cancers, overweight and obesity, gastrointestinal (GI) diseases, fatty liver, depression, and cognitive decline. It is positively associated with better quality of life, good sleep, and healthy lipid profiles, which support heart health.
- In children, the anti-inflammatory diet is associated with less overweight and obesity, improved cardiovascular and respiratory fitness, less asthma, improved academic performance, less sensory processing abnormalities, less ADHD, less fatty liver, less functional GI disorders, better mental health, and better overall quality of life.

In short, eating anti-inflammatory foods is an important way to maintain good health and prevent illness. It can also be used as part of a broad approach to treat chronic diseases linked to inflammation, including many of those previously listed.

THE ANTI-INFLAMMATORY WAY AND CULTURAL EATING

While research on the Mediterranean and Okinawa diets is impressive, these are certainly not the only two healthy dietary patterns in the world—they're just closely studied ones. In fact, when we broaden our view, we can see that many traditional diets, which are very different in flavor and preparation, share core tenets that make them anti-inflammatory. We believe that every traditional diet has its own nutritional wisdom and that there is no *one* anti-inflammatory way. Instead, there are anti-inflammatory principles that can be adapted to any family's culture, no matter your ethnicity or the flavors you are drawn to.

A lot of attention has been focused on the portrayal of cultural traditions in the food media. Issues include chefs and food writers laying claim to the traditions of others, failing to honor the expertise and labor of those steeped in the cuisine being discussed, or adding "inauthentic" shortcuts or ingredients to make traditional foods more accessible, to name a few.

We believe it's important to be transparent about who we are and how we approached the recipes in this book. Each of us brings our individual cultural experiences to this book, intertwined with and also independent of our ethnicity. Maria is an integrative pediatric gastroenterologist and nutrition expert who grew up in India. Her pantry is never without ginger, turmeric, garlic, and other freshly ground spices. Stefania is the child of Sicilian immigrants whose palate and kitchen skills were shaped by her grandmothers—and by an abundance of tomatoes. She is also a chef and herbalist who helps families adapt their traditional recipes to the specific nutritional and health needs they might be facing, like food allergies or gut-related illnesses. Hilary is also a first-generation American, the child of Scottish immigrants, and her favorite flavonoid-rich beverage is a cup of Irish breakfast tea. As an integrative health pediatrician, she works to translate the powerful science of anti-inflammatory diet into real and tasty meals that her patients (and her own family) will enjoy. Jon, the descendant of Eastern European Jews from Ukraine and Hungary, grew up on Ashkenazi classics at holidays. Tired of the "heart-healthy easy weeknight dinners" he was raised on (aka overcooked boneless, skinless chicken breasts), he taught himself to cook by watching after-school cooking shows on PBS. Ally traces her passion for cooking to her German great-great-grandparents, who had a bakery in northeast Philadelphia. She has explored the cuisines of many countries through travel and studied cooking in Crete, Greece, whose rich cuisine is credited with residents' exceptional longevity.

As far as our recipes are concerned, you may bristle that few of them are "authentic"—and we would agree. Tofu with saag? Eggplant in shakshuka? Fennel Slaw on Fish Tacos? We didn't aim to record with perfect fidelity traditional recipes as they are known in each culture. We did choose to include dishes that are influenced by a multitude of cultures because we want to emphasize that anti-inflammatory foods are found in every cuisine—and not just those that have been most studied, like the Mediterranean diet. Our goal is not to highlight traditional recipes—plenty of cookbooks do that already. Rather, the over one hundred recipes in this book reflect those we have enjoyed cooking and eating with our friends and families, and which have become part of *our* traditions. We don't claim that they are "*the most* anti-inflammatory," or that recipes from cultures we didn't represent should not be included. On the contrary! We recognize that you bring your own expertise to the table. We come at this project to share but also to learn. We hope that, like any good cookbook, it's a spark for your imagination and a conversation starter. To that end we invite you, readers, to share your own anti-inflammatory family recipes on our website www.seedtotable.org. Share something that is authentic to your table, or tell us how you changed one of our recipes to your liking. We welcome all skill levels, background, cultures, and ages to participate!

WILL MY CHILD EAT ANTI-INFLAMMATORY FOODS?

For many parents, this is the most pressing question. Our simple answer is yes, of course they will! Children learn to eat foods that are part of the families and cultures in which they are raised. Think of hot chili peppers in India, raw fish and seaweed in Japan, and bitter dandelion greens in Italy. These are not easy flavors we were born loving. But as children are repeatedly exposed to these foods, they become favorites. These children even grow into adults who crave these foods and teach their children to embrace them. Training children's palates to enjoy healthy foods is a well-worn path and absolutely worth the effort. Studies show that establishing positive eating habits in childhood paves the way for a lifetime of good health, especially in combination with the other core components of wellness—physical activity, positive social support, restful sleep, and effective stress management. Chapter 3 will lay out a road map for how to successfully introduce anti-inflammatory foods to your children, even the pickiest ones. But first let's talk about the building blocks of the anti-inflammatory way.

BUILDING BLOCKS OF THE ANTI-INFLAMMATORY WAY

The basic components of the anti-inflammatory way are simple and can be summed up in a few broad guidelines:

1. **The anti-inflammatory way considers the context of how you eat your meals.** It isn't just about what's on your plate, but also the context in which you eat. Do you enjoy your food? How fast do you eat? Are you enjoying your food mindfully or gulping it down while you watch TV or send texts? Whom do you eat with and what kind of conversations are happening at the table? Can you recognize your own satiety (fullness) cues? Mealtimes are opportunities to introduce a whole mindset about food and nutrition that will stick with your kids throughout their lives. As adults, we have a responsibility to be positive and creative role models. This is not just a wise old adage; the supporting research is strong!

2. **The anti-inflammatory way is "plant-forward."** This does not mean vegetarian (though the anti-inflammatory way can easily be adapted to a vegetarian diet). It does mean that you will eat more foods from plant sources than animal sources, including a wide variety of vegetables, fruits, legumes, whole grains, nuts, seeds, herbs, and spices. Plant foods are the most concentrated

sources of the nutrients our bodies need to keep inflammation low. Animal foods, like fish, eggs, yogurt, cheeses, and some meat are also part of the anti-inflammatory way, but in smaller quantities than in the typical American diet. More on this in Chapter 2.

3. **The anti-inflammatory way is based on whole (and preferably organic) foods.** This means that foods are minimally processed and as close to their natural state as possible. Whole foods have a full spectrum of nutrients that keep inflammation in check, as opposed to most processed foods, which increase inflammation. In addition, there is increasing evidence that some food additives, such as artificial coloring and flavoring, are harmful, especially to children. Many processed foods are also high in sugar, which is pro-inflammatory. Preferably, the whole foods you choose are also seasonal, local, and organic where possible.

4. **The anti-inflammatory way incorporates healthy fats from a variety of sources.** Like most traditional diets, the anti-inflammatory way is not low-fat. The latest science has shown that good fats are absolutely necessary for healthy growth, especially for children. The key is to pick the right kind of fats. Some fats have been shown to be anti-inflammatory allies, while others cause cell damage and inflammation. In particular, the anti-inflammatory way emphasizes using fats from nuts and seeds like olive oil and sesame oil, as well as oily fish, which have important omega-3 fatty acids.

EATING CONTEXT: SETTING THE STAGE FOR HEALTH

The anti-inflammatory way is about much more than a list of foods that should be eaten or avoided. Eating is a cultural act, shaped by centuries of biological, agricultural, and social traditions. It's not only about nutrition; it's also about family, pleasure, and celebration. We embrace the pleasure of hearing onions sizzle in the pan, of filling our homes with the aroma of spices that wrap us in familiarity, and of indulging in a sweet treat that we may not need nutritionally but certainly appreciate psychologically. Food is a symbol as well—a carefully presented lunchbox can remind your children of your love for them even when separated by the time and distance of the school day.

Key to the anti-inflammatory way is remembering the powerful emotional and social connections food can bring. For many families, mealtime, and particularly weeknight dinners, can correspond with a stressful time of day. Kids are "hangry," parents have not shaken off their work stress, and there is still much to be done—homework for kids (and often adults); clubs, sports, or other evening activities; household chores—and all with an eye on the clock for a good night's sleep. It is no wonder that in this environment food becomes something to be dealt with rather than something to be enjoyed. We may seek the convenient, cost-effective, or craveable option in service of our schedules rather than investing the effort to cook a meal in the anti-inflammatory way.

What is required here is a reframing. We may not be able to use food to mitigate the stresses of work, school, and other obligations. But we can remember that foods prepared in an anti-inflammatory way can be convenient, cost-effective, and make everyone feel good psychosocially, as well as physically. As an example, frozen or store-bought pizza is a stress night staple for many families. The burden is on the parents to feed the kids. An anti-inflammatory reframe of this scenario is to make our Vegetable Pita Pizzas. Adults lay out the ingredients and give kids the responsibility to "decorate" the pizzas with their favorite vegetable toppings, thereby shifting some of the burden and choice of dinner from parents to kids. Serve alongside a salad, and you have a much healthier (and equally fun) dinner in about 20 minutes.

How you experience the dining table is also part of the anti-inflammatory way. We are not advocating unrealistically long, leisurely dinners. We are saying, however, that being present—off the phones and tablets, looking at one another and not a screen, sharing stories, and being thoughtful about the food and its flavors—has both nutritional and psychosocial benefits. Nutritionally the evidence is clear that eating while distracted, often by an electronic device or TV, results in mindless eating and overconsumption beyond satiety cues. It also adds to the noise, stress, and distraction that make the convenient, ultra-processed foods so appealing in the first place. Lots of good research shows that children who eat meals in a positive, social family setting are more likely to be a healthy weight and consume a healthier variety of foods.

Finally, children can and should be active participants in meals. Throughout the book, you'll find recipes that make especially fun cooking activities with kids. But you don't need to wait for a special recipe or occasion to get kids involved in the kitchen. Chapter 5 will provide tips for how to involve kids as young as three years old in daily meal prep. Research consistently shows that when children get involved in meal planning, cooking, serving, and even cleaning up, they are much more likely to be adventurous and healthy eaters. And they develop critical skills they can use for life.

PLANT-FORWARD

The typical American diet is woefully low in plant foods compared to traditional diets from around the world. Plant foods are vegetables, fruits, legumes, whole grains, nuts, seeds, and herbs and spices. Each year, nutrition experts recommend we eat more plants, and each year we fall short. One core goal of this book is to help you fall in love with plant-based foods through delicious recipes. This section will explain why plants are the foundation of the anti-inflammatory way.

Fiber

One of the nutrients that is only found in plant foods is fiber. You've probably heard plenty about the benefits of fiber. Maybe your pediatrician has told you that your child needs to "eat more fiber." What this really means is "eat more plants" because fiber is a substance found *only* in plant foods. Simply defined, fiber is the indigestible parts of plant foods. But why would something that you can't digest be so good for you? It's complex, and we don't know all the reasons. But here are some things we do know:

- **Fiber slows digestion to a healthier pace.** When fiber-rich plants are a substantial portion of your meal, your food gets digested more slowly and more thoroughly. This means that you feel full more quickly (reducing the amount of food you eat) and stay satiated longer (reducing the amount of snacking between meals). Slower digestion also stabilizes blood sugar levels. Reducing "sugar highs" is very important for children's physical, mental, and behavioral health. Keeping blood sugar (and insulin) levels steady is one of the best ways to reduce inflammation.

- **The friendly microorganisms that make up your microbiota thrive on fiber during the digestive process.** Once you have extracted nutrients in the early phase of digestion, the gut microbiome finishes the job. In fact, for some beneficial microbes, these prebiotic fibers are their preferred meal. For example, when your microbiota eat them, they release something called short-chain fatty acids (SCFAs), which are potent anti-inflammatory compounds. In turn, SCFAs become food for other cells in your gut. Fiber is an integral part of this virtuous cycle—it feeds your microbiome, and your microbiome feeds you. This is absolutely critical because a healthy microbiome is essential to developing and sustaining a healthy immune system and the healthy level of inflammation.

In sum, a diet high in fiber (i.e., plant foods) reduces inflammation in the gut and throughout the body. It helps you maintain a healthy weight and stabilize blood sugar and insulin and allows your microbiome to make anti-inflammatory compounds when fiber is broken down and digested.

Phytochemicals

For many years, nutrition science was focused mostly on the importance of macronutrients in food, of which there are three: proteins, fats, and carbohydrates. In the first half of the twentieth century, scientists started to understand that food was made up of a much fuller picture when they discovered micronutrients that are essential to health, including vitamins, like vitamins A, B, and C, and minerals such as calcium and magnesium. More recently, the picture has gotten even richer as researchers have begun to focus their attention on thousands of other micronutrients that are neither vitamin nor mineral but are now understood to regulate the inflammatory processes that are at the core of our health. The greatest abundance of these anti-inflammatory micronutrients is found only in plants.

These compounds can go by many names, including phytochemicals (*phyto* means "plant"), polyphenols, and antioxidants. These are largely interchangeable terms.

Polyphenols are present in all plant foods and are especially concentrated in fresh vegetables and fruits, herbs and spices, legumes (such as peas, beans, lentils, soybeans, and peanuts), coffee, and teas. More than 8,000 different polyphenols have been identified and grouped into classes based on their chemical makeup. Among these, flavonoids are probably the most studied type of polyphenols and are the most abundant in the human diet—so far, we've identified more than 4,000 of them! Flavonoids account for the vibrant colors of flowers, fruits, and leaves of many plants and are concentrated in brightly colored plants such as berries, dark leafy greens, sweet potatoes, and tomatoes.

The reason polyphenols are referred to as antioxidants is because of one of the mechanisms by which they help us. They protect against oxidation caused by free radicals, which is harmful to our cells. Free radicals are also known as reactive oxygen species. They are dangerous because they float around the body looking to "grab" oxygen molecules from the DNA, proteins, and fats that make up the membranes and insides of our cells. This leads to cell damage, which can then lead to cancer, cardiovascular disease, diabetes, osteoporosis, and some neurodegenerative diseases.

Like inflammation, oxidation is a normal human process that occurs all the time. And, also like inflammation, oxidation can increase to unhealthy levels when we are exposed to excessive environmental stressors like unhealthy foods, pollutants, and emotional stress. This is where plant antioxidants come in. You can think of them as the buffers, donating their own electrons to the free radicals, thereby decreasing oxidative damage. Polyphenols, and especially flavonoids, are great antioxidants. Interestingly, when plants are more stressed (because of too much wind, sun, or drought, for example), they make more flavonoids to protect themselves. In turn, when people eat plants, we receive protection from physiological damage driven by the stressors of life.

Phytochemicals in plant foods also directly influence our cells and genes to turn inflammation up or down. Chronic inflammation is like a runaway response of the immune system, which can seemingly take on a life of its own. It pushes the immune response into overdrive, upregulating (turning up) inflammatory mediators, which in turn signal other cells and body systems to rev up the inflammatory cascade. You may have heard of some of these pro-inflammatory compounds, such as cytokines, prostaglandins, and nuclear-factor kappa B (NF-κB).

However, there are also compounds that redirect these pathways, signaling cells to dial down inflammation. For example, one such powerful compound goes by the long name NF-E2-related factor-2 (Nrf2). A central job of Nrf2 is to cool down inflammation and promote actions that protect your cells and genes.

As it turns out, plants are extraordinarily rich in phytochemicals that activate anti-inflammatory Nrf2 and inhibit pro-inflammatory compounds like NF-κB. Many of these compounds have been closely studied, including curcumin, which is found in turmeric; isothiocyanates found in cruciferous vegetables such as broccoli, cabbage, cauliflower, and kale and collards; and anthocyanins, which are found in deep red and purple food like berries, grapes, cherries, and eggplant skin.

These are just some of the complex mechanisms by which phytochemicals communicate with your cells to protect your health. This is an area of active and exciting research. In the meantime, the message is crystal clear: Eat more plants!

WHOLE FOODS

The anti-inflammatory way emphasizes a whole-foods approach because these offer the health benefits of a broad spectrum of beneficial micronutrients lost during commercial food preparation. Ideally, foods will have undergone minimal to no commercial processing, which is not only healthier but also reduces environmental pollutants generated in the processing and packaging process.

Processing is not inherently bad. In fact, it can be beneficial to a safe, scalable, and convenient food supply. We're not suggesting that you begin each day by milling your own flour or fermenting your own tea. What we're really talking about is steering away from ultra-processed foods. For example, rolled oats are a lightly processed food. You begin with whole oats, which are dehusked, steamed, dried, and rolled. This is perfectly consistent with the anti-inflammatory way. By contrast, many packaged cereals are heavily processed. Typically, grains used in cereals are first refined, which eliminates the vast majority of fiber and nutrients. Then they may get powdered; mixed in a slurry with sugar, salt, flavors, and preservatives; extruded through a die; infused with artificial colors; baked; and finally placed inside both a plastic sleeve and a cardboard box (which often contain their own preservatives). This is far from a whole food.

The Evidence Against Food Additives

Equally important as the good things whole foods contain is the stuff they *don't* have, including colorings, preservatives, and other food additives. In 2018, the American Academy of Pediatrics (AAP) issued its first-ever policy statement warning of the harmful effects of processed foods and packaging on children's health. The AAP reviewed and highlighted the growing research on the detrimental impact of food additives (coloring, flavoring, and other chemicals), as well as the substances that come into contact with food during processing and packaging (adhesives, dyes, cardboard, plastics, and other chemicals). Many of these substances have been shown to have serious health effects, including increasing inflammation, interfering with insulin metabolism, negatively impacting the microbiome, and disrupting the hormones in children's endocrine systems.

Children are especially vulnerable to the impact of these additives because they eat more food per pound of body mass than adults, and because their bodies and brains are still developing. The AAP raised special concern about the effects of additives on children's endocrine systems, noting that hormones regulate the function of all parts of the body, and even small disruptions at important moments in development can have permanent, lifelong consequences.

When it comes to additives that are inside food, reading ingredient labels carefully is the best way to avoid them. Identifying which chemicals are in food packaging is considerably more difficult because they are usually not named in food labels, and it's hard to find accurate information in other ways.

FOOD ADDITIVES

Here is a list of the top food additives you may find in processed foods. Note that these are just a few chemicals among hundreds. Science is still emerging on their health consequences.

ADDITIVE	SOURCE	FUNCTION	FOUND IN
High fructose corn syrup	Corn	Enhance sweetness	Many cookies, crackers, icings, and other desserts and soft drinks
Trans fats	Partially hydrogenated vegetable oils; also may be in mono and diglycerides	Improves shelf life	Cookies, crackers, margarines, and other processed foods
Sodium nitrites and nitrates	A salt-like product naturally found in some vegetables	Help stabilize, color, and flavor meat; prevent bacterial growth	Cured meats such as bacon, hot dogs, and lunch meats
Sulfites (sulfur dioxide, potassium bisulfite, sodium bisulfite, or sodium sulfite)	Synthetic; also naturally present in some foods like black tea	Preservative	Dried fruits, fruit juices, wine, pickled foods, molasses, dried potatoes, wine vinegar
Food colorings (e.g., FD&C Yellow #5 and #6, Red #40)	Synthetic	Adds color	Candies, cereal, and other processed foods
BHT and BHA	Synthetic antioxidant	Preservative, especially to increase shelf life of oils	Butter, meats, cereal, chewing gum, baked goods, snack foods, dehydrated potatoes, beer, food packaging

ADDITIVE	SOURCE	FUNCTION	FOUND IN
Benzoates	Synthetic; also naturally present in berries, seafood, milk products	Inhibits growth of bacteria and fungi	Fruit pies, jams, beverages, salad dressing, relishes, sauerkraut
Carrageenan	Made from red seaweed	Thickener and emulsifier	Ice cream, yogurt, cottage cheese, soy and nut milks, processed foods
Monosodium glutamate (MSG)	Made by fermenting starch, sugar beets, sugar cane, or molasses	Enhances flavor and texture	In soups and other processed foods like salad dressings, frozen dinners, chips, and some Asian packaged foods
Gums: guar, xanthan, and locust bean gum	Guar gum: fiber from guar plant Locust bean: fiber from carob plant Xanthan gum: synthetic; made by mixing corn or other sugars with fermenting bacteria	Thickener and binding agent	Gluten-free products; dairy; salad dressings; cosmetics
Ascorbic acid	Vitamin C	Antioxidant that is used as a preservative	In many processed foods, including baby food

CHEMICALS IN FOOD PACKAGING
This is a list of just a few of the chemicals found in packaging materials and the negative health consequences with which they have been linked.

CHEMICAL	FOUND IN	LINKED TO
Bisphenols, like BPA	Plastic containers, including some with recycling number 3 or 7 Linings of aluminum cans (though many manufacturers have removed them)	Obesity; ADHD; acts like the hormone estrogen and can interfere with puberty and fertility; interacts with immune and nervous systems
Phthalates	Plastic packaging and tubes and storage containers; also garden hoses, inflatable toys, nail polish, hair sprays, lotions, and fragrances	Acts like a hormone; interferes with male genital development; increases risk of obesity and cardiovascular disease
Perfluoroalkyl (PFC)	Grease-proof paper, cardboard packaging, nonstick pans, and water-repellent fabrics	Can lead to low-birth-weight babies; causes problems with immune system, thyroid, and fertility
Perchlorate	Used in some packaging to prevent static	Interferes with thyroid function and disrupts early brain development

Tips for Avoiding Additives and Chemicals

- The single best way to avoid additives and chemicals in food packaging is to eat mostly whole foods and reduce processed foods.
- Read ingredient labels carefully. Whatever you don't recognize, look up!
- Use alternatives to plastic (such as glass or stainless steel) for storing food. If you do use plastics, avoid putting very hot food in them and avoid putting them in the dishwasher or microwave. For example, don't microwave infant formula or breastmilk in plastic bottles.

- Look at the recycling code on the bottom of plastic products and avoid plastics with recycling codes 3 (phthalates), 6 (styrene), and 7 (bisphenol/BPAs). If plastics are labeled as "biobased" or "greenware," that's generally okay—it means they are made from plant material and do not contain BPAs.

Sugars

Refined sugars are in many processed foods. This includes obvious foods such as cakes and candy, as well as less obvious foods such as salad dressings, sliced breads, and flavored yogurt. To say that sugar and inflammation are linked is a big understatement. Researchers have established a highly complex relationship between sugar intake, insulin, adipocytes (fat cells), fructose metabolism, gut microbiota, pro-inflammatory cytokines, and metabolic diseases such as diabetes and heart disease. A detailed review of this science is beyond the scope of this book, but here are a few important takeaways for families:

- First, excess sugar intake is linked to an increased risk of developing obesity and insulin resistance. When you eat sugar, glucose enters your bloodstream and, in response, the pancreas releases insulin. Insulin's job is to "knock on the door" of cells and compel them to take the extra glucose out of the blood and into cells, where it can be used for energy. This is a healthy, adaptive mechanism. Glucose is the primary food your cells need to function. However, when the body is faced with excess sugars and refined carbohydrates, the system gets overwhelmed. The cells stop responding as well to insulin—although it is always knocking! This is a simplified explanation of insulin resistance, and if left unchecked, it can lead to type 2 diabetes, a disease whose prevalence has climbed steeply in children. In one decade, between 2002 to 2012, the rate of new diagnosed cases of type 2 diabetes in youth increased by 4.8 percent each year. Furthermore, chronically elevated insulin levels drive systemic chronic inflammation.
- Second, sugar impacts behavior and mood. This is especially noticeable in children. Quite soon after you eat sugary food, blood sugar levels spike and you feel that proverbial sugar high. The sweet taste is intimately connected with your

body's pleasure and reward mechanisms, including your opioid circuitry, endo-cannabinoid system, and even your serotonin levels. Eating sweet foods releases endorphins, the feel-good chemicals that are also stimulated by vigorous exercise or opioid drugs. Researchers, including the former head of the FDA, David Kessler, have made the case that, because of this chemical effect, sugar has addictive properties. It hijacks your reward centers, makes you feel good (temporarily), and leaves you craving more so you can experience that feeling again.

The kind and quality of sugar matters. Complex sugars, which are found in whole foods such as fruits, sweet vegetables like sweet potatoes and beets, and whole grains like brown rice, also have fiber and many other nutrients. Fiber slows the release of sugar into the bloodstream, thereby tempering its effects on insulin and mood. The recipes in the dessert chapter of this book (Chapter 12) are based on these whole and naturally sweet foods. Occasionally, we also use some added sweeteners in our recipes, like honey, maple syrup, and even sugar. That's okay! We're not suggesting you need to eliminate sugar altogether. But do pay close attention to limiting it.

The American Heart Association and the American Academy of Pediatrics recommend staying within these limits (and we encourage you to stay well under them):

- No added sugars for infants and children up to two years old
- Less than 6 teaspoons per day for children up to eighteen years old (half that amount for children in the younger part of that age range)
- Less than 6–10 teaspoons per day for adults (depending on size)

Those seem like reasonable numbers, right? Well, the average American adult consumes 34 teaspoons per day of added sugar, and for children, it's 19 teaspoons per day!

On nutrition labels, sugar is listed in grams, not teaspoons. But there is an easy formula to convert grams to teaspoons so you can better visualize how much sugar is in each product; 4 grams of sugar is about 1 teaspoon of sugar. Or, let's put it another way:

$$\text{Total grams of sugar} \div 4 = \text{Teaspoons of sugar}$$

Most sugar is hidden in processed products, but the greatest source of that excess sugar is not even from food—it's from sugary drinks. These include sodas, sports drinks, energy drinks, fruit drinks, sweetened coffees and teas, and even vitamin waters. While occasional sweet treats are just fine as part of the anti-inflammatory way, regular consumption of sugary beverages is not. For many Americans, the easiest way to reduce sugar is simply to cut out sweet drinks. The beverage recipes in this book can help you transition off these drinks and enjoy health-supportive alternatives.

SNEAKY SUGAR SYNONYMS

Sweeteners go by a lot of different names in ingredients lists!
Here are some to watch out for:

- Anything with the word "sugar," such as brown sugar, beet sugar, coconut sugar, invert sugar, raw sugar, and so on
- High fructose corn syrup and corn syrup
- Anything with "ose" at the end, like fructose, sucrose, maltose, glucose, and dextrose
- Anything with "malt," like barley malt, malt powder, or ethyl maltol
- Anything with the word "cane," like cane sugar or dehydrated cane juice
- Anything with the word "saccharide," like fructooligosaccharide
- Anything with the word "syrup," like maple syrup, oat syrup, rice syrup, and so on
- Fruit juice concentrates such as grape or apple concentrate
- Maltodextrin
- Molasses
- Honey

Artificial Sweeteners

Finally, there are artificial sweeteners, which are widely used in diet beverages and other low-calorie processed foods like ice cream, desserts, cereals, and chewing gum. The three most common are saccharin, aspartame, and sucralose. All of them remain under active study to understand their effects on human health, including their links to liver damage, behavioral and cognitive issues, negative effects on the microbiome, and cancer. We recommend avoiding them altogether, especially for children. A better choice for a no-calorie sweetener is stevia, a natural sweetener extracted from the *Stevia rebaudiana* plant, which originates in South America and is related to the daisy. Stevia is approximately two hundred times sweeter than sugar. A tiny pinch can lend ample sweetness (though too much will lend bitterness).

Even if artificial sweeteners are safe to eat, there is another big problem with them: They condition our palates to love sweet food. Many health-promoting foods like greens, fermented foods, or good fats have bitter or sour components. If we condition our palates to love sweetness through sugar and artificial sweeteners, it becomes harder to embrace the more "difficult" flavors found in healthful ingredients.

ARTIFICIAL SWEETENERS
These are the three most common artificial sweeteners and the health concerns with which they are associated.

Artificial Sweetener	Concerns
Saccharin (pink packets)	Remains under study for possible detrimental effect on healthy gut bacteria, normal immune function, and overall health
Aspartame (blue packets)	Associated with liver damage in animal studies and remains under active study for other health concerns including cancer and behavioral and cognitive issues; can cause migraines, hives, seizures, and allergic reactions; contraindicated in people with phenylketonuria (PKU)
Sucralose (Splenda) (yellow packets)	Remains under study for possible detrimental effect on healthy gut bacteria, normal immune function, and overall health

ORGANIC

Along with eating whole, plant-based foods, the anti-inflammatory way prioritizes organic foods. The USDA certifies organic foods that are grown in compliance with rigorous federal guidelines covering soil quality, methods for pest and weed control, animal raising guidelines, and use of additives, among other factors. Produce labeled "organic" must be grown on soil that is certified to be free of prohibited substances for three years prior to harvest. This includes use of synthetic fertilizers and pesticides, among other things. Organic meat must be obtained from animals raised with access to the outdoors, fed 100 percent organic feed, and never given antibiotics or growth hormones. Packaged and processed organic foods must be free of artificial preservatives, dyes, and flavoring. The USDA organic label specifically bans use of any genetically modified foods or components.

Although purchasing organic foods may not be feasible all the time, prioritizing certain food groups eaten frequently, such as produce, dairy, and eggs, can be beneficial. This is important, as research shows that synthetic pesticides and fungicides, antibiotic-treated meats and poultry, and artificial additives in processed foods are harmful to children and adults. The research includes alarming findings for children exposed to pesticides, such as the following: decreased cognitive function and increased behavioral problems (including ADHD), cancer, and birth defects. Research on glyphosate, one of the most ubiquitous pesticides, has also found association between prenatal exposures and autism disorder. These examples are really just the beginning when it comes to the concerning health effects related to pesticide exposure in children. The American Academy of Pediatrics recommends that based on the weight of scientific evidence, children's exposures to pesticides should be as limited as possible. Since eating and drinking have been shown to be the primary ways most children are exposed to pesticides, purchasing organic foods where possible helps protect them from harm.

For produce, each year the Environmental Working Group (EWG) puts out a list of the "Dirty Dozen" and "Clean Fifteen" based on data on pesticide residue collected by the USDA. On their most recent list, the EWG Dirty Dozen (the ones with most pesticide residue) were strawberries, spinach, kale, nectarines, apples, grapes, peaches, cherries, pears, tomatoes, celery, potatoes, and hot peppers. In addition, we recommend prioritizing organic dairy, eggs, and meat. In animal-based foods such as these, not only are pesticides a concern, but so are the antibiotics that are routinely fed to animals.

Local and Seasonal

The anti-inflammatory way also emphasizes local and seasonal eating. These two concepts, local and seasonal, go hand in hand. Each ecosystem has its own rhythm. If you live in a climate with four distinct seasons, many fruits and vegetables are in their peak season only in the summer months. In more moderate climates, you may find the same vegetables growing nearly all year long. For example, if you live on the East Coast of the United States, avocados and oranges are never "in season" because they can't grow there. That doesn't mean you need to avoid these foods. The anti-inflammatory way recommends eating locally and seasonally where possible, with flexibility based on what's available to you.

Eating locally and seasonally can confer a number of benefits. It encourages you to eat diverse foods (and therefore a variety of nutrients) year-round. It connects you to local farmers, leading you to establish a personal connection both to the people and the land that produce your food. It means you are supporting preservation of farmland around where you live, which positively impacts air quality and your access to nature. It helps support local economies and educates children (and adults) about nature, climate, and agriculture. Finally, it can be cost-effective, as peak-season produce is often a good value.

HEALTHY FATS

Fats are a very important component of food. They've been given a bad rap, but good fats are an essential part of our diets. Without fat, you are unable to fully absorb fat-soluble vitamins essential to your health, such as vitamins A, E, D, and K. Fats also form the building blocks for hormones and for the membranes of your cells. The kind of fats you eat determines to a great degree the health of each and every one of your cells. Children in particular need enough fat because it helps with their development and growth, especially of their brains. Of course, fats also impart flavor and texture to your food and help you feel satiated.

Like most traditional diets (including the Mediterranean and Okinawa) the anti-inflammatory diet is not "low-fat." Instead, the anti-inflammatory way emphasizes choosing high-quality, whole fats in moderation. Because of the importance of fat intake in the developing brain, children in particular should not be given low-fat products, including low-fat dairy. The science on fats is rich and always evolving, but we will simplify it here so you can make good choices for your family.

There are three types of fats: unsaturated, saturated, and trans fats.

Unsaturated Fats

Unsaturated fats are found most abundantly in plant sources, like nuts, seeds, and some fruits, like avocados and olives. In oil form, they are liquid at room temperature. Perhaps you've heard that unsaturated fats are the healthiest kind. This is, in part, true. High-quality unsaturated fats help reduce inflammation, build stronger cell membranes in the body, and improve blood cholesterol levels, which can decrease risk of heart disease and type 2 diabetes. However, some oils that have mostly unsaturated fats are highly inflammatory. Let's break this down so you can make informed choices.

In a nutshell, the quality of oils is based on both their source (what kind of nut, seed, or fruit it comes from) and the processing it undergoes (how it gets from a nut, fruit, or seed to an oil). For example, organic extra-virgin olive oil and highly refined corn oil are both unsaturated, but they are not equally healthy choices. The former helps to keep inflammation low, while the latter is pro-inflammatory. Why? Extra-virgin olive oil is made through a process that is called "expeller-pressed" or "cold-pressed." This means that the oil is extruded from the olive with just the weight and force of a large press. The press squeezes the olives and out comes the oil. In contrast, highly refined oils, including corn, soybean, and blended oils sold as "vegetable oil," are made through a process that has many steps. First, oil is extruded from the seeds with chemical solvents, including hexane. The oil is then heated to very high temperatures, which removes most of the (toxic) hexane, but also removes many of the oil's own anti-inflammatory antioxidants. Heating oil to these high temperatures also creates carcinogenic substances and free radicals, which are pro-inflammatory. Finally, the oil goes through an "RBD" process—refined, bleached, and deodorized. This yields an oil that is flavorless and nearly colorless and has a very high smoking point so it can be used for frying. It also yields a very poor-quality fat that promotes inflammation. We do not recommend using these highly refined oils in your home. Also, limit eating fried foods like French fries, onion rings, fried chicken, or fish in restaurants, as they are probably using one of these oils. Here's the bottom line: Choose oils that say "expeller-pressed," "cold-pressed," or in some cases "virgin" (like extra-virgin olive oil). If possible, also choose organic oils.

Unsaturated fats can further be broken down into two categories: monounsaturated and polyunsaturated fats. Many foods contain a mixture of these two in differing ratios, so it's almost impossible to say that a food is only one or the other.

Monounsaturated Fats

Monounsaturated fats are found in high ratios in olives and olive oil, avocados and avocado oil, as well as a wide range of nuts and seeds and the oils made from them, such as safflower, sunflower, canola, and grapeseed oil.

Polyunsaturated Fats (or Essential Fatty Acids)

Polyunsaturated fats have a special feature: They are also called "essential fatty acids," which means that we cannot make them in our bodies and must get them from food. There are only two essential fatty acids: omega-3 fatty acid (aka alpha linolenic acid) and omega-6 fatty acid (aka linoleic acid). While both omega-3 and omega-6 fatty acids are important, we need to pay attention to the *ratio* between them. The typical American diet has much more omega-6 than omega-3 fatty acids. These mainly come from refined vegetable oils such as soybean and corn oil, as well as from meats. In the anti-inflammatory diet, we seek to flip that ratio, emphasizing omega-3 over omega-6 fatty acids. This is because omega-3 fatty acids have been found to be more anti-inflammatory and very beneficial for good physical and mental health. Omega-3s are found most prominently in fatty fish, such as wild salmon, mackerel, sardines, and anchovies, as well as plant sources such as ground flaxseed and flaxseed oil, nuts and nut oils (especially walnuts), and chia seeds—all ingredients you will find sprinkled throughout our recipes.

Saturated Fats

Saturated fats are mainly found in animal sources like meats and dairy products but are also found in some plant sources such as coconut and palm oils, which are solid at room temperature. While we often think of saturated fat as synonymous with meat, in reality most animal products are a combination of saturated and unsaturated fats. Eggs, chicken, dairy, and red meats all contain a combination of saturated and unsaturated fats.

The bottom line with saturated fats is that they can be part of a healthy diet in moderation, but generally not as beneficial as *high-quality* unsaturated fats. Too much saturated fat in the diet has been correlated with negative long-term health outcomes in some people, including many types of cancers and cardiovascular disease.

The recipes in this book use meat, dairy, and coconut oil in moderation, and we recommend that you do too.

Trans Fats

Trans fats occur naturally in some foods in small amounts. But the vast majority of trans fats in today's diet are made through a food processing method called partial hydrogenation. These fats are highly pro-inflammatory, increase bad (LDL) cholesterol and triglyceride levels, and lower good (HDL) cholesterol levels, thus increasing the risk of heart disease. They are not essential and have no known health benefits. With growing awareness of the health risks these fats cause, food manufacturers have eliminated them from many foods in recent years. However, they may still be found in some margarines, shortenings, and many processed foods, including crackers, cookies, ready-made frostings, and others. Look for the words "partially hydrogenated" in the ingredients list and avoid them!

Cooking with Fats

Finally, how you cook with fats can influence their impact on health and inflammation. Some fats are best used cold, in salads or drizzled on bread or vegetables. Others can withstand moderate heat, including baking and sautéing. The simple rule is to apply moderate instead of high heat to oils to avoid reaching their smoking point (the temperature at which oil emits smoke). When that happens, it releases carcinogens and makes free radicals, which are pro-inflammatory. See the Foods Rich in Healthy Fats section in Chapter 2 for lots more detail about choosing and cooking with healthy fats.

THE ANTI-INFLAMMATORY WAY AND THE MICROBIOME

This chapter would not be complete without further discussion of the human microbiota (or microbiome), a fast-moving area of medical research. Changes in microbiota have been observed in nearly *every* disease, including all the chronic and mental health conditions linked to inflammation. Researchers have only just begun to unlock the complex relationship between the quality of your microbiota and the quality of your health. While research is changing rapidly, there are a few fundamentals that are important to understand.

Let's start with some definitions. The human *microbiota* is all the microbes that live on and inside the human body, including bacteria, fungi, protozoa, and viruses. The *microbiome* is all the genetic material of these microbes. The relationship between you and your microbes is, under healthy circumstances, mutually beneficial. They help you to digest your food, protect against harmful microbes (pathogens), and produce vitamins your body needs, and they play a key role in regulating your immune, GI, endocrine, and nervous systems. Research on the microbiome reinforces the complex ecology of the human body.

The infant microbiota is significantly influenced during birth. If babies are born through a vaginal delivery, they primarily take on the microbiota of their mothers. If instead they are born by C-section, they largely take on the microbiota of the people and environment immediately around them in the hospital, which is less beneficial. Thereafter, everything the child is exposed to affects the composition of his microbiota, including food, medicines (especially antibiotics), and environment.

While those early years are critical in shaping the composition of your microbiota, even the adult microbiota adapts quite quickly based on what you eat. For example, within days of transitioning to a diet richer in plant foods, you can observe changes in the gut microbiota. Overall, studies have shown a more diverse microbiome is associated with greater health. People who eat a variety of foods, and *especially* a diet rich in plant foods, have a more diverse microbiome.

In addition, both probiotic and prebiotic foods are especially good for your microbiome. Probiotic food contains live, beneficial microbes, which are achieved through a process of fermentation. Some examples are yogurt, kefir, kombucha. tempeh, miso, and many different kinds of fermented vegetables such as sauerkraut and kimchee. These ingredients are sprinkled throughout our recipes and are easy to incorporate into your daily diet. For example, stir a teaspoon of miso into salad dressing, add some sauerkraut to a salad or sandwich, and add a dollop of yogurt to oatmeal. In general, it's best if these products are eaten raw, not heated, which can kill the live organisms.

Prebiotic foods are those that contain nondigestible plant fibers that your microorganisms like to eat. Not all plant fibers are considered prebiotics, but *many* different plant foods have them. For example, onions, garlic, bananas, broccoli, asparagus, beans and peas, seaweeds, whole wheat, oats, chia, barley, and so many more! As long as you eat a wide variety of whole plant foods, you'll get lots of good prebiotics that will benefit your microbiota. If you feed them plant foods, they grow and thrive. They, in turn, create a diverse and resilient environment in your gut, which is essential for a strong immune system, healthy inflammatory response, and good mental health.

SUMMARY: TIPS FOR EATING THE ANTI-INFLAMMATORY WAY

- The context of your meals really matters. Relaxed, social, and screen-free meals support good health.
- Eat an abundant variety of plant foods, which includes vegetables, fruits, whole grains, legumes and beans, and nuts and seeds.
- Eat mostly whole, unpackaged foods. This is the best way to avoid harmful additives in food and on packaging. Learn to recognize the names of additives, especially the many words for sugars, so you can avoid them.
- Choose organic where possible. This limits your exposure to harmful pesticide residues and supports environmental health.
- Incorporate high-quality fats in your meals, including enough omega-3s, and tailor your choice of fats to the cooking method.
- A plant-rich, whole-foods diet that includes probiotic (fermented) and prebiotic foods supports a diverse microbiome, and a diverse microbiome is essential to your overall physical and mental health.

CHAPTER 2

The Anti-Inflammatory Family Food Table

This chapter will bring you on a journey through the Anti-Inflammatory Family Food Table, a visual guide to help you navigate food choices. While shopping and menu planning, you're faced with a lot of questions and decisions. What's the difference between organic, free-range, and conventional eggs? What fish is healthy to eat? How can I identify whole grains? Is soy good for me and my kids? This chapter will tackle these questions and lot more. Before diving into these specifics, let's step back and look at the big picture.

GUIDING YOUR FAMILY'S FOOD DECISIONS

The details of food choices are certainly important, but it's equally important not to get overly stressed about them. Keep these three high-level points in mind to guide your family's food decisions.

- **Balance science with culture.** The recommendations in this book are based on the latest science. But science is always changing. So, we balance science with commonsense wisdom learned from the world's food traditions. Look back at how people in your culture ate generations ago, when the incidences of chronic, diet-related diseases were much lower than today. This table is meant to be flexible. Shape it to the cultural and health needs of *your family*.

- **Variety and moderation.** There is no "magic bullet" to healthy eating. Be skeptical of claims of "superfoods," which overstate the benefits of one food instead of a whole diet. The best way to eat healthfully is to eat a variety of real, whole foods (especially plant foods). Likewise, too much strictness around eating is unhealthy! Occasional treats are welcomed at the table—just remember to enjoy them fully and in moderation.

- **Plants, plants, plants.** Take a moment to notice that the bottom three-fourths of the anti-inflammatory food table is exclusively plant foods: vegetables, fruits, seeds, nuts, grains, and legumes. Plants take up so much space on the table because they are anti-inflammatory powerhouses that protect your family's health. Also, eating more plant than animal foods is essential for a healthy planet, which we will explain in more detail later. The environment you live in plays a strong part in determining your inflammatory burden. Healthy earth means healthy families.

HISTORY OF THE ANTI-INFLAMMATORY TABLE

In the late 1990s, Dr. Andrew Weil created an Anti-Inflammatory Food Pyramid, which was adapted from the US Department of Agriculture food pyramid, but provided a substantial shift from its recommendations. This new pyramid combined a foundation of recognized anti-inflammatory foods

Pediatric ANTI-INFLAMMATORY FOOD TABLE

Healthy Sweets
occasional

Foods Rich in Healthy Fats

Dairy & Calcium-Fortified Dairy Alternatives

Protein-Rich Animal Foods

Protein-Rich Plant Foods

Whole Grains & Noodles

Herbs & Spices

Vegetables & Fruits
of varied colors

Water & decaffeinated tea
unlimited

CHIA

SOY

MILK

YOGURT

MILLET

BARLEY

QUINOA

OATS

RICE

© H.H. McClafferty, MD, FAAP

Image Credit: Hilary McClafferty

in the Mediterranean and Asian diets. In 2011, Dr. Hilary McClafferty (one of the coauthors of this book) developed the Pediatric Anti-Inflammatory Food Pyramid especially for children. Also, in 2011, the USDA switched from the food pyramid to a plate shape called MyPlate, and the Harvard School of Public Health amended it to come out with their own Healthy Eating Plate. These plates provide a simple visual recommendation to "make half your plate veggies and fruits," which we fully support.

The Anti-Inflammatory Family Food Table you see here is an updated version from 2020 that serves as a visual guide to the anti-inflammatory way for the whole family. McClafferty's shift from pyramid to table sends another important message: Eating is a communal and social activity, meant to be enjoyed together at a common table.

WATER

We begin with water, the go-to beverage for families eating the anti-inflammatory way. In Chapter 1, you learned that sugar-sweetened beverages are one of the largest sources of dietary sugar for both adults and kids. Just *one* soda, energy drink, or sweetened coffee or tea typically exceeds a whole day's total of recommended added sugars for adults—and *way* exceeds the limit for most kids. For example, a 12-ounce can of Coca-Cola has nearly 10 teaspoons of sugar! During meal and snack times, put a pitcher of water on the table. You may like to add slices of fruit such as orange, lemon, or strawberries, and/or fresh herbs such as basil and mint for flavor and color. Seltzer or sparkling water are also great choices, as long as they are unsweetened.

TEA

Enjoying teas daily is a great way to add powerful anti-inflammatory compounds to your diet. Basically, the word "tea" means any beverage made by infusing a plant in water. The two main categories of tea are (1) those made by infusing the tea plant *Camellia sinensis* (these are usually referred to as "tea"), and (2) those made by infusing herbs, which are referred to as "herbal teas" or "tisanes."

Black, green, oolong, and white teas have very different flavors, colors, and aromas. But they all originate from the same plant—*Camellia sinensis*. The difference is in the processing. Black teas are fermented, oolong is partially fermented, and green tea is not fermented; rather, it is processed in other ways, such as steaming. While all teas have antioxidants, green teas and white teas have the most. Green teas are particularly famous for one category of polyphenols, called catechins, which research shows are highly anti-inflammatory and can have beneficial effects against cancer, diabetes, and cardiovascular diseases. It has even been shown to help reduce gum disease and other periodontal problems, which are important indicators of systemic inflammation in both children and adults.

What about Caffeine?

All tea from the tea plant has caffeine, which we do not recommend for children, as they can be much more sensitive to its effects than adults. Caffeine may interfere with sleep, which is critical for healthy development. For school-age children, choose herbal teas or decaffeinated teas. When buying decaffeinated teas, check the label to see how they are processed. Some use a solvent called ethyl acetate, which removes caffeine but also removes most of tea's beneficial polyphenols. The better method, called "CO_2 processing" or "effervescence," uses just water and carbon dioxide and retains most of the polyphenols.

For adults, coffee can also be part of the anti-inflammatory way. It, too, is high in antioxidants, but also much higher in caffeine, which is not indicated for children.

Herbal Tea

The other main category of tea is herbal tea. Herbal teas can be made with hundreds of different plants, such as lemon balm, tulsi, lavender, licorice, mint, ginger, and even with mushrooms like reishi, or grains like barley. Cultures around the world have rich traditions of using herbal teas as medicines, both to prevent illnesses and to treat them. Herbs can be effective for everyday ailments like bellyaches, insomnia, mild anxiety, colds, and sore throats. When you are able, prioritize buying organic herbs and teas.

VEGETABLES AND FRUITS

Vegetables and fruits hold the most privileged place in the anti-inflammatory table—bottom and center. They are *the* foundation of the anti-inflammatory way. As a reminder, the reason vegetables and fruits are so important is because they have fiber and a huge array of phytochemicals that interact with your cells and genes to regulate inflammation.

Vegetables are not a botanical category but a culinary one. What we call a vegetable actually includes many different parts of plants, such as the stem (celery, asparagus), leaves (all leafy greens), flower (broccoli and cauliflower), roots (carrots, turnips), bulbs (onions, garlic), tubers (potato, yam), seeds (edamame, peas), or seed pod (string beans, snap peas). Sometimes what we think of as a vegetable is actually a fruit, like tomatoes, squash, and cucumbers. That's okay—they are welcomed in the vegetable category too! If you find that your children don't love vegetables, we devote much of Chapters 3 and 4 to helping you turn that around.

Botanically, fruits are the edible reproductive part of a plant that has seeds. The seeds can be in the core, like apples and peaches, or distributed throughout, like bananas or raspberries. This part of the plant is usually sweet and is designed to be delicious so that animals will eat it and spread its seed. Note that fruits have many of the same benefits as vegetables, including fiber and anti-inflammatory phytochemicals. But they are higher in sugar, so they occupy a smaller space than vegetables on the table.

Here are tips for maximizing the anti-inflammatory benefits of vegetables and fruit:

- **Eat a rainbow of colors.** Phytochemicals are expressed in part through color, so eating a variety of colors is one way to ensure you are getting a variety of anti-inflammatory nutrients. The deeper the color, the better—like orange squash, red beets, dark green kale, and blueberries.

- **Where you can, buy organic produce.** Don't peel it (but do clean before eating). Many of the nutrients and fiber are concentrated in the skins.
- **Choose produce that is in season and local.**
- **Prepare vegetables and fruits in a variety of ways.** Eat them both cooked and raw—these impart different benefits. Cooked are more easily digested, while raw preserves more of the delicate nutrients.
- **Include fermented vegetables, like sauerkraut, kimchee, and fermented pickles.** These provide valuable probiotics for your microbiome, which plays a big role in regulating inflammation.
- **Don't forget about sea vegetables.** Seaweeds, such as nori, hijiki, and dulse, are some of nature's richest sources of minerals.
- **Fruits are nature's best dessert!** Many cultures end their meals with a piece of fruit to satisfy the desire for something sweet. Adopt this simple habit in your house. On special occasions, try one of the many fruit-based recipes in our desserts chapter (Chapter 12).
- **Minimize fruit juice consumption.** The American Academy of Pediatrics recommends not serving juice at all to children under two years old and infrequent servings to older kids. Unlike whole fruits, fruit juice does not have fiber. The detrimental effect of juice on blood sugar is very similar to that of refined sugars, which are found in sodas. If serving juice at all, the healthiest way is to dilute it with water or seltzer (see the Juice Spritzer recipe in Chapter 13).

Mushrooms

While mushrooms are a fungus, not a plant, we include them in this layer because they are often treated like vegetables in cooking. Here are some tips for mushrooms:

- Choose Asian mushrooms like shiitake and maitake over button mushrooms whenever possible. They are packed with anti-inflammatory and anticancer nutrients and, like many herbs, are considered a medicinal food throughout the world.
- *Always* cook mushrooms of any kind. Cooking breaks down toxins that may be found in raw mushrooms.

HERBS AND SPICES

Although herbs and spices are typically used in small quantities in recipes, they have a privileged place in the anti-inflammatory pyramid because of the frequency with which we encourage you to use them. They are also largely responsible for a food's cultural and flavor footprint. Like vegetables and fruits, they should take a lead role in every meal! Generally speaking, herbs are the leaves of aromatic plants, fresh or dried (such as rosemary, bay leaf, parsley, or cilantro) while spices are other parts of the plant like seeds, roots, or bark (like cinnamon, nutmeg, allspice, or pepper).

Herbs and spices are nature's *most potent form of anti-inflammatory compounds*. Indeed, they were people's original medicine. Their intense colors, fragrance, and flavors give us a peek into their potency. Some, like turmeric, have now become famous for their anti-inflammatory qualities. But many more are similarly powerful, including basil, parsley, rosemary, cilantro, oregano, cloves, garlic, ginger, cumin, cinnamon, coriander, and paprika.

WHOLE GRAINS

In the whole-grains category, you will find many of the world's staple crops, such as wheat, rice, corn, oats, rye, barley, millet, teff, amaranth, and quinoa. Most of these are considered "true" grains, which means they come from grasses. Others, like quinoa, amaranth, and buckwheat, come from plants other than grasses. But this distinction doesn't really matter. What they have in common is they are seeds, and you eat them in similar ways. Seeds are a special part of the plant because they hold what a plant needs to make new life. Here are two rules for incorporating grains into the anti-inflammatory table:

1. Choose whole grains.
2. Eat a variety of whole grains. Wheat is by far the most consumed grain in America. Add variety by including new grains like amaranth, millet, and barley.

As with fruits and vegetables, each grain has different nutrients, and variety ensures that you're eating a wide spectrum of anti-inflammatory compounds.

What Are Whole Grains?

The anti-inflammatory table emphasizes eating whole grains instead of refined grains. What's the difference? Whole grains contain three layers (see diagram): The bran, which is the outermost layer and contains fiber, B vitamins, and minerals; the germ, which is a small part of the seed that is super packed with nutrients, including antioxidant and anti-inflammatory compounds; and the endosperm, which is mostly carbohydrates and some protein.

By contrast, refined grains contain only the endosperm. This means that

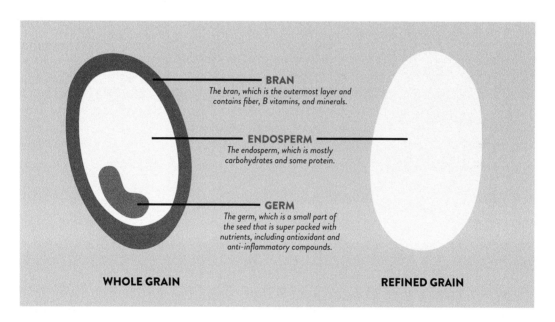

they lack most of the fiber and anti-inflammatory nutrients. They become pure starchy carbohydrate, which can spike and then decrease your blood sugar levels, similar to simple sugars, and can drive inflammation.

How can you recognize what is a whole grain and what is refined? Whole grains come in a few different forms:

- **Seeds:** For example, brown rice, whole-wheat berries, quinoa, millet, corn kernels, and amaranth.
- **Rolled:** "Rolled" grains are just whole grains that have been steamed and then rolled or flattened; for example, rolled oats, rolled rye, or quinoa flakes. These are great because they cook quickly!
- **Flour and whole-grain products:** Whole grains can be made into flour. For example, whole-wheat seeds make whole-wheat flour, and whole oats make oat flour. The flour is used in many different products, such as whole-wheat pasta, bread, or crackers. To identify these, the words "whole wheat" or "whole grain" must be the *first* ingredient listed on the package. Even "100 percent wheat," "natural grain," or "minimally processed" *do not* mean whole grain.

"White" or Refined Grains

Everything that doesn't fall into those previous categories is refined. These include white rice and anything made from all-purpose flour, such as noodles, cereals, bread, crackers, pastries...and the majority of junk foods! Eat these foods sparingly.

What about Gluten?

Gluten-free diets are increasing in popularity. Gluten is a protein in wheat, rye, spelt, and barley. For those who have celiac disease, a wheat allergy, or sensitivity to gluten, eliminating gluten-containing foods is essential. There is also some evidence that gluten-free diets can help people who have irritable bowel syndrome, rheumatoid arthritis, psoriasis, and some other disorders. Research is ongoing in this area; talk with an informed health practitioner for guidance if you are considering a gluten-free diet for yourself or your children.

For the majority of people, however, there is strong evidence that wheat and gluten do not lead to inflammation or health problems. They can absolutely be part of a healthy, well-rounded diet. In fact, many gluten-free products are considerably less healthy than whole-wheat products. They will often include fillers, gums, and other additives. If you do choose gluten-free products, read labels carefully!

What about Rice and Arsenic?

Research has raised concerns about the amount of inorganic arsenic in rice. *Inorganic arsenic* is a naturally occurring compound, but also one found in increased levels in soil due to pollution from mining, pesticides, and fertilizers. In large quantities, it has been linked to serious health conditions like some cancers, heart disease, and more. Many foods absorb arsenic from soil, but rice takes up more than most.

Arsenic poses the greatest risk to infants, children, and pregnant women. This is because infants and children have a greater food intake per body mass ratio than adults, and their bodies and brains are still developing. Arsenic also passes through the placenta to the fetus. Rice and rice flour are used in many products for infants and children, such as infant rice cereals, energy bars, rice pasta, packaged cereals, and in many gluten-free foods.

While this information sounds scary, your family definitely doesn't need to stop eating rice. You may absolutely still eat it in moderation. Here are some practical tips for how to eat it healthfully:

- **Eat a variety of grains:** Grains like amaranth, buckwheat, millet, and cornmeal have almost no arsenic, and bulgur, barley, and farro have very little.
- **Vary infant cereals:** Consider alternatives to infant rice cereals, such as oat, barley, or multigrain cereals.
- **Cooking method:** Rinse rice several times before cooking and discard rinse water. Then, instead of cooking it with the steaming method, where all water is absorbed, cook it in a 6:1 ratio (6 cups water, 1 cup rice) and drain excess water before serving. You can remove a good amount of the arsenic in this way.

- **Type of rice:** According to *Consumer Reports*, white basmati rice from California, India, and Pakistan, and sushi rice from the US have on average half of the inorganic-arsenic amount of most other types of rice. Also, although brown rice is generally healthier because it is a whole grain, it has more arsenic than white rice. Moderating intake of both is the wisest course.

In addition, it's important to realize that organic rice is not necessarily free from arsenic. Arsenic stays in the soil for many decades, so even rice that is grown on a field that is organic today may absorb it. However, organic rice is grown without the addition of harmful pesticides and fertilizers.

PROTEIN-RICH PLANT FOODS

The next level of the anti-inflammatory table consists of plant foods that are especially rich in protein, which includes legumes, beans, nuts, and seeds. Many of us grew up with the idea that protein is found primarily in foods that come from animals or fish. In reality, if you choose to do so, you can get all the protein your body needs from plants.

Legumes

Legumes are a large family of plants that includes beans, lentils, and even peanuts. The world of legumes is big, colorful, and very diverse. Just in the bean category, there are *thousands* of different kinds! Some of the most popular are black beans, pinto beans, and chickpeas, but many heirloom varieties are making a comeback. Beans range from very small, like the tiny green mung bean from India, to quite large, like the Greek butter bean aptly named gigantes. Lentils are also very diverse—red, yellow, green, black, and colors in between. Beans and lentils are at the center of anti-inflammatory cuisines from around the world and are featured in many of the recipes in this book!

Soy

Soybeans are also legumes. They deserve special mention because of the privileged place they hold in many East Asian diets. They can be eaten whole (steamed edamame) or made into tofu, tempeh, miso, soy sauce, and many more products. Here are important tips for including soy in a healthful way in your family's diet:

- **Choose organic:** In the 1960s, only about 20 percent of soybean acres were treated with pesticides, but today it is near 100 percent. In fact, one-fifth of all pesticides used in the US are used to grow soybeans. Choosing organic is the only way to avoid these pesticides.
- **Eat in moderation:** Soy is promoted by some as a wonder food, and by others as a phytoestrogen to be avoided. Both positions are exaggerated and untrue. Soy has been eaten healthfully in East Asia for many generations. Eat it in moderation, like most everything else.
- **Choose soy products wisely:** The healthiest soy products are relatively unprocessed, like tofu. Some others, like tempeh and miso, go through a process of fermentation, which brings even more benefits. Stick with these "real" soy products and stay away from heavily processed soy, which is often found in packaged foods. This includes soy isolates, soy lecithin, textured vegetable protein, and more.

FISH

Fish and shellfish are excellent sources of protein, vitamins such as B_{12} and D, and a variety of beneficial minerals. Some are also excellent sources of omega-3 fatty acids, including mackerel, sardines, herring, trout, and salmon. The diets that the anti-inflammatory way is based on, including Mediterranean and Asian diets, have seafood (especially the smaller, omega-3-rich fish) on their table two to three times per week.

Choosing the healthiest fish for your family is not a simple topic. There are three main issues to think about, which we will explain in the following section.

While the issues are complex, rest assured that there are very good resources that can help you navigate these choices.

- **Choose fish with low mercury content.** Pollution and contamination of waters from coal and other industrial plants significantly impacts the quality of fish, including increasing its methylmercury content. Methylmercury is a metal that has detrimental health effects on the human nervous system and is of particular concern for women who may become pregnant or are pregnant, as well as infants and children. Larger fish, such as tuna, shark, and swordfish, usually have the highest levels of mercury. (See the National Resource Defense Council guide that follows.)
- **Choose fish whose populations have not been overfished.** Today, this is a very significant environmental problem. We urge you to consult the following Monterey guide for guidance.
- **Wild or farmed?** The practice of aquaculture, or fish farming, is steadily growing. It has gotten a bad rap, in large part because many fish farms use harmful practices like putting antibiotics and other chemicals in feed. But newer practices are improving a lot. Many are clean, meticulous about the feed and nursery environment, and yield nutritious and safe seafood. Aquaculture will need to be part of the solution to meet global demand without overfishing an already depleted ocean.

Here are two great resources to help you make decisions:

- National Resource Defense Council Smart Seafood Buying Guide: www.nrdc.org/stories/smart-seafood-buying-guide. It rates high-, medium-, and low-mercury fish and has other good suggestions.
- Monterey Bay Aquarium Seafood Watch app. Download and bring it with you to the market. It is a detailed and up-to-date guide on the most and least sustainable seafood, including how they are caught or farmed, and whether they are overfished.

PROTEIN-RICH ANIMAL FOODS

On the anti-inflammatory table, animal-based foods are on a relatively small square. This means that families eat meats, dairy, and eggs in moderation instead of frequently. Why? There are two interrelated reasons:

1. **Your family's health:** Diets that are heavy in animal products are linked to greater inflammation, a less diverse microbiome, and decreased overall health. Studies have linked red meat consumption with increased risk of obesity, inflammation, and cancer.

2. **The world's health:** Animal-rich diets are simply not healthy or sustainable for the world. And we can't have good individual health in a world that is not healthy. Unfortunately, the production of animal-based foods contributes to major public health problems, especially climate change and antibiotic resistance.

Climate Change

Agriculture is responsible for over 25 percent of the world's greenhouse gas emissions, and animal foods make up the overwhelming majority of this percentage. In particular, two red meats—beef and lamb—are the biggest culprits. For example, the production of beef emits more than 27 times the carbon dioxide than the production of lentils. In addition, the production of animal foods uses much more water than plant-based foods. Beef is by far the most water-intensive, using on average 1,847 gallons of water per pound of meat, compared to 718 gallons per pound for chicken, and 302 gallons per pound for tofu.

Antibiotic Resistance

In the US 80 percent of all antibiotics are used not on humans but in animal agriculture. This is done to marginally increase growth rates and keep down infection, which otherwise occurs frequently because of the cramped conditions animals are held in. When animals are given small and constant doses of antibiotics, bacteria adapt and can become antibiotic resistant. Antibiotic-resistant bacteria can then spread to and infect humans. According to the CDC, an average of 2.8 million people in the US become infected and at least 35,000 die from antibiotic-resistant bacterial infections annually.

Following we have tips to help your family incorporate eggs, meats, and dairy into your meals in a way that is good for both you and the world.

Eggs

Eggs are a nutritious food filled with protein, vitamins, and minerals. They have a lower environmental impact compared with meat and cheese, and are economical. For many years, recommendations said to limit egg consumption because their cholesterol content could theoretically increase risk of cardiovascular disease. But many recent studies have overturned that wisdom and shown that moderate egg intake (up to one egg per day) does *not* increase blood cholesterol or the risk of cardiac disease.

Buying high-quality eggs is important—but the number of choices can be overwhelming. Let's look at what various labels mean:

- Most eggs (about 97 percent) in the US are from chickens held in small cages that hold five to ten birds. Each bird has less space than a piece of printer paper. This is neither humane nor healthy.
- "Cage-free" means that the chickens are not held in cages and are allowed to move around, but only indoors.
- "Free-range" means the chickens are cage-free and also have access to the outdoors. However, because facilities are very large, this might mean they have *potential* instead of actual access to the outdoors.
- "Organic eggs" must be both cage-free and free-range. Chickens are fed an organic diet and not given any antibiotics.
- "Omega-3 enriched" means that chicken's feed is being supplemented by flax or fish oils to increase their omega-3 fats.
- "Pasture-raised." Unlike the previous labels, pasture-raised is not a label certified by the USDA. It is instead regulated by Certified Humane, which requires

at least 2 square feet per bird and 6 hours of outdoor space, where they can engage in their natural behaviors, including foraging for plants and insects.

Where possible, buy organic or, even better, pasture-raised eggs. Not only is the nutritional quality of these eggs better, but it also discourages the terrible mistreatment of chickens. At home, one way you can judge the nutritional quality of eggs is by cracking an egg. Ideally, the yolk should be deep yellow orange (rather than pale yellow) and should be round and high instead of flattened.

Meats

The anti-inflammatory way treats meat as a special-occasion food, not an everyday food. Here are some tips for how to incorporate meat healthfully onto your family's table:

- **Use small amounts to increase flavor.** Meats and cheeses are deeply flavorful, and a little goes a long way. For example, in our Creamy Chicken Soup, we use only one-eighth pound of chicken per serving, but because the meat flavors a whole soup, and then gets shredded into small pieces, it's really satisfying. Dishes that lend themselves well to this technique are soups, stews, stir-fries, pasta, casseroles, burritos, and many more!
- **Make it 50 percent beans.** Whenever you use ground meat, as in burgers, meatballs, or tacos, mash 50 percent beans into it. In addition to adding fiber and phytochemicals, this "stretches" the meat, making it more affordable. For example, try the Meatball and Escarole Soup recipe in Chapter 9.
- **Choose chicken and turkey over beef and lamb.** Poultry has a much smaller carbon and water footprint than red meat.
- **Choose organic or grass-fed.** The USDA "organic" label tells you that animals have been fed with organic feed, raised on organic land, raised without antibiotics or added growth hormones, and have outdoor access year-round. The USDA "grass-fed" label means that cows must be fed grass and other greens, rather than grains. There is evidence that beef from organic or grass-

fed animals has more omega-3 fatty acids and more antioxidant vitamins, such as vitamins A and E.

Meat substitutes are another issue. These substitutes such as the Beyond Burger, Impossible Burger, and many others are increasing in popularity. These meat substitutes are usually made with a fairly long list of non-whole-foods ingredients. From the perspective of personal health, if you choose to eat them, they go into the "occasional" food category. A better choice is to try our Black Bean Burgers recipe in Chapter 8. But on the whole, are meat substitutes better for the earth than meat? Definitely.

Dairy

Although many people feel that a meal is not complete without a glass of milk to accompany it, milk and dairy are not nutrition "must-haves." But in moderation, dairy can be a nutritious, delicious part of your family's anti-inflammatory table. Two things you've likely heard about dairy: It's necessary because of its high calcium content, and low-fat dairy is better than high-fat. Let's look at these two claims.

- **Calcium.** While calcium is an important nutrient, it is not necessary to eat dairy to get enough of it. It is also found in plant foods such as tahini; tofu; dark leafy greens like kale, broccoli, and collards; and sea vegetables. Alternative milks, such as almond and soy, are usually fortified with calcium as well.

- **Low-fat or full-fat?** Contrary to USDA advice, multiple studies now show that choosing low-fat over whole milk does *not* help with weight control or cardiac health in children or adults. In fact, several studies in children indicate that full-fat dairy might confer more health benefits and help regulate weight. Eating full-fat dairy leads to a greater feeling of satiation, and if we pay attention to those cues (which children are thought to be naturally good at), it can help us maintain a healthy weight.

These guidelines can help you incorporate dairy into your family's anti-inflammatory table:

- Prioritize fermented dairy, like plain, whole milk yogurt and kefir, which feed your microbiome!
- A little cheese goes a long way. Use a sprinkle to boost the flavor of otherwise plant-based meals, like our Vegetable and Bean Chili (see Chapter 9).
- Choose organic milk, yogurt, and cheese whenever possible (or at least rBGH/rBST-free). Organic dairy ensures that your family is not getting residual growth hormones, pesticides, and antibiotics, and also reduces these harmful chemicals in the environment.
- Choose full-fat dairy (especially for children) and pay attention to satiety cues.

FOODS RICH IN HEALTHY FATS

One of the things that sets the anti-inflammatory table apart from many other food models is our emphasis on the importance of eating foods rich in healthy fats. These foods take up a small space on the table because with fats, a little goes a long way. Remember from the discussion in Chapter 1 that the *quality* of fats matters! Choose oils that say "cold-pressed," "expeller-pressed," or "virgin," and whenever possible, choose organic.

Some of the best sources of anti-inflammatory fats:

- Extra-virgin olive oil, which is consistently linked to low inflammation
- Avocados and olives
- Ground flax seeds and flax seed oil
- Whole nuts and seeds, such as almonds, walnuts, pistachios, pumpkin seeds, sesame seeds (including tahini), chia seeds, and more
- Oils from some expeller-pressed nuts and seeds like sesame, walnut, sunflower, safflower, grapeseed, or avocado
- Fish rich in omega-3s, such as wild salmon, mackerel, and sardines

Sources to use in moderation:

- Eggs (preferably organic)
- Whole dairy (preferably organic), such as yogurt
- Butter or ghee
- Coconut oil
- Meat (preferably organic and/or grass-fed)

Sources to avoid:

- Trans fats, which may be found in margarine, shortening, or processed foods
- Highly refined vegetable oils, such as corn, soybean, peanut, canola, or blended oils often called "vegetable" oil

Cooking with Fats

It's important to choose the right fat for the cooking method so you avoid reaching the fat's smoking point. If you are cooking on a stovetop, keep the heat low enough so the oil doesn't smoke. Use this chart to help guide your choices:

COOKING METHOD	TYPE OF FAT TO USE
For salad and other no-heat recipes	Extra-virgin olive oil Flaxseed oil Walnut oil Sesame oil, toasted or untoasted
For baking (up to 350°F) and cooking (under the smoking point, which varies for each oil)	Extra-virgin olive oil (use mostly) Sesame oil, toasted or untoasted Avocado, sunflower, safflower, or grapeseed (use these when you need a more neutral taste than olive or sesame oil) Butter, ghee, or coconut oil
For high-heat cooking (use very sparingly!)	Refined avocado, sunflower, or coconut oils

HEALTHY SWEETS

On the smallest rung of the table are healthy sweets. Desserts please your palate and can bring joy. They are welcomed on the anti-inflammatory table, as sometimes-treats. The recipes in this book are based on whole, naturally sweet, anti-inflammatory ingredients like fruits, whole grains, and yogurt. One that deserves special mention is dark chocolate. Chocolate is made from the cacao plant, *Theobroma cacao*. The name *Theobroma* is derived from Greek, meaning "food of the gods," and the plant has a long history in many culinary traditions. Raw and unrefined cacao beans are very high in antioxidant polyphenols. On their own, they are also quite bitter, so sugar is added to make them more palatable. To benefit from the anti-inflammatory properties of these health-protective compounds, choose dark chocolate, preferably 70 percent cacao or higher. This maximizes the cacao and minimizes the sugar.

To add sweetness to muffins, cookies, and cakes, we also use honey, maple syrup, and, more rarely, Sucanat. Like white sugar, Sucanat comes from cane, but is less refined than white sugar, retaining some molasses and trace minerals. Keep in mind that while these sweeteners are less refined than white sugar, all sweeteners act similarly in the body, spiking blood sugar and bringing on a surge of insulin that can increase inflammation. No matter the kind of sweetener, it is important to use in moderation!

SUMMARY: THE ANTI-INFLAMMATORY FAMILY FOOD TABLE

- Eat a wide variety of foods. This is the best way to get a variety of nutrients your body needs and minimize the negative impact of eating too much of one thing.
- Treat these guidelines flexibly, adjusting them to your family's culture and food preferences.
- Mirror the anti-inflammatory table by making three-fourths of your table plant foods—vegetables, fruits, whole grains, legumes, nuts, and seeds. And don't forget cooked mushrooms!

- Incorporate healthy fats into every meal, leading with the most anti-inflammatory.
- Invite seafood onto your table a couple of times per week, focusing on small, sustainable fish that are rich in omega-3 fats.
- Enjoy eggs, meat, and dairy in moderation and be mindful of how they impact the earth's resources.
- Educate yourself about the environmental impacts of your family's food choices. What's good for the earth's health is good for your family's health!

CHAPTER 3

Expanding Your Child's Taste Preferences

Encouraging children to eat a varied and healthy diet can be one of the most challenging aspects of child-rearing for parents. In this chapter, we will walk you through the biological, developmental, psychological, and cultural factors that influence taste development in children. And we will give you strategies for expanding your child's palate. These strategies are culled from best practices in two important areas—traditional ways of eating and scientific research—which often align. These strategies have worked to transform children from fussy eaters into mature, intrepid eaters in many cultures and over generations, and they can guide you to success in your home as well.

RESISTANCE IS NORMAL, DON'T DESPAIR!

You are likely to encounter some form of resistance to foods you offer to your children. It may be mild and infrequent, or it may feel constant and fierce. It will change over time, both from one day to the next and over the years. Your child may make faces, push your hand away, close her mouth in resistance, tell you that she will *never* eat green things, and employ a variety of other exasperating strategies to reject the delicious meal you worked hard to prepare. There are many reasons for this behavior, including inborn taste preferences, fear of the new, and the normal developmental process of individuation that all children experience. This chapter will explore some of these behaviors to help provide insights into the underlying reasons for your child's reactions.

There are three important takeaways that can help you succeed in expanding your child's food preferences. First, the mealtime struggles you may face with your child are a normal part of development. They are as common and as predictable as the trial and error that comes with learning to walk and talk. With a few good practices and patience, you can feel assured that they will also be temporary.

Second, because food struggles are a universal part of child-rearing, parents do not need to reinvent the wheel in coming up with strategies to overcome them. Many cultures have made an art out of instilling healthy eating habits in children, and grandmas all over the world have a great deal of wisdom to share in this arena. Many of these practices are also backed by significant scientific research. The bottom line is children have a very flexible palate. They learn to eat the foods of their families across every culture and cuisine, and your child, too, can learn to love a varied diet full of delicious, healthy foods.

Third, teaching children to eat healthfully entails work and patience and is well worth the effort. Childhood presents a unique window of opportunity for developing food preferences and eating behaviors. "Picky eating" is a term that sounds innocent enough, but it can severely restrict diet at a time when children need a wide variety of nutrients to support growing bodies and brains. It may have negative health outcomes, such as low iron and constipation, and lead to increased stress, anxiety, and family conflict. The time and energy you invest early on will set the foundation for your child's good health well into adolescence and even adulthood.

THE BIOLOGY OF TASTE

From birth, babies show an aversion to some tastes (namely, bitter) and desire for others (sweet). Studies show that if you give newborns a drop of a bitter substance on their tongues, they grimace in rejection. If you give them a sweet substance, they make faces of satisfaction and enjoyment. In addition, children have a different level of sensitivity to the bitter and sweet flavors than adults do. Children are *more* sensitive to bitters than adults. That means they will detect the flavor even if there's not much of it in a particular food. For example, while many adults may think of carrots as on the sweet side, children may perceive more of their underlying bitterness. At the same time, children are *less* sensitive to sweet flavors than adults—that is, they will gravitate toward much more concentrated sweetness.

It's worth pausing to examine the bitter flavor in particular because it helps us to understand the "problem" with kids and vegetables. While all foods are made up of a nuanced combination of flavors, plants have more bitterness on the whole than animal foods. This is true of vegetables, nuts, seeds, and even of fruits to some degree. Think of the bitter kick in walnuts, coffee, or even in the skin of a carrot. The reason plants have more than their fair share of bitterness has to do with evolution. Unlike many living things, plants are stationary. They can't run away from predators or find a shady spot when the sun gets too strong. Their main defense, therefore, is through chemicals, specifically phytochemicals. To deter deer and caterpillars from munching on their leaves, plants ramp up their bitter chemicals, which in high doses can be toxic to these predators. For humans, these same phytochemicals in the plants are not toxic. On the contrary—they can be some of the most health-protective compounds we can eat, *essential* to our good health! As with the antioxidants we introduced in Chapter 1, it turns out that many of the phytochemicals that plants use to protect themselves also protect us. But for children, who have evolutionary warning signals embedded in their tongues, the bitter flavor can be a tough sell.

In the first four to six months of life, children's sensitivity to bitterness rarely causes problems because breastmilk and formula are both predominantly sweet. But when children begin to eat solid foods, these biological taste preferences can show up as rejection of vegetables and greater acceptance of sweeter foods, such as grains and fruits. In addition, neophobia, or fear (phobia) of the new (neo), can appear at this time, a well-documented stage of development that causes children to be highly skeptical of new foods. For parents trying to raise healthy eaters, the confluence of these factors can generate significant anxiety.

But—*and this is an important but!*—innate flavor preferences at birth actually play only a small role in our eventual taste preferences. The process of learning, through what we are exposed to and what people around us eat, plays a much bigger role in influencing our taste preferences. Just as children's bones lengthen to accommodate growing tissue, and their minds develop infinitely greater capacities, their tastes are highly plastic—they are designed for change. And the way they change is through what child nutrition experts call "exposure," or what we can think of as *relationship building*.

TASTE DEVELOPMENT IN PREGNANCY AND INFANCY

Like all of us, your relationship with food begins in utero. Your taste and smell receptors begin to form at seven to eight weeks of gestation, and by around twenty weeks of gestation, fetuses even begin swallowing small amounts of amniotic fluid. Compounds called aromatic volatiles, which are found in all foods, are dissolved and carried in amniotic fluid. In this way, the amniotic fluid that bathes the fetus is perfumed with the aromas of foods the mother has ingested. We can imagine this as a rich sensory experience for the fetus—like smelling under water. A similar process is true of breastmilk. It, too, takes on the aromas and flavors that the mother has ingested. Studies show that just a short time after the mother eats garlic, vanilla, or other highly fragrant foods, breastmilk noticeably takes on those flavors.

Unsurprisingly, once babies are weaned, those who are exposed to particular foods in utero and through breastmilk show a preference for the foods and beverages their mothers have ingested. Familiarity breeds comfort. For example, one study showed that if mothers drank carrot juice during pregnancy or breastfeeding, their children were much more likely to accept carrots when they were introduced to them in solid form as compared to children of mothers who avoided carrots. Overall, several studies have shown that children who are breastfed are less picky and more accepting of new foods than those who are not—and that this benefit can last for many. This makes sense, since breastfeeding exposes infants to a wide variety of flavors on a daily basis, while formula has a uniform flavor.

INTRODUCING SOLID FOODS

Whether children are breastfed or formula-fed, repeated exposure continues to be the path of learning once infants are introduced to solid foods. Let's clarify what we mean by "exposure" at this age. It doesn't mean that your child must eat a full helping of a particular food at first. It does mean that your child sees the food, smells it, touches and explores it with her hands, tastes a little bit of it, hears positive words about it, and sees the people around her enjoying it. All of these interactions count as positive experiences that build familiarity and help overcome neophobia.

You may want to think about introducing new foods in the same way as you think about any other developmental skill your child will learn. She will try many times (definitely more than five) to stand up and take her first steps before succeeding, but you certainly wouldn't give up on helping her walk! All those previous attempts are not failures. They're just practice and preparation for success. Like any practice, it proceeds bit by bit and can come with frustration. A few guidelines can help.

First, expose babies to a variety of foods early. Most experts agree that babies should be introduced to solid foods at around six months. Some signs that they are ready include sitting with little or no support, good head control, and opening their mouth and leaning forward when food is offered. The right timing will depend on the individual needs of your child, so discuss it with your pediatrician. During the time when babies are first introduced to solid foods, which is called the "complementary feeding" period, they should still get the majority of their calories from breastmilk or formula. Therefore, it's a great time to let your child engage with new foods purely for the sake of curiosity and exploration, and with no pressure.

Second, expose babies to a wide variety of both flavors and textures, especially during the complementary period and up to two years old, when studies show they are most receptive. The greater variety of flavors they experience, the more willing they are to embrace new flavors in general. For example, introducing squash, carrots, and spinach one day can lead babies to more readily accept a vegetable they've never seen, like green beans, the next day. Novelty becomes normalized. Therefore, aim to offer a variety of foods in every meal, especially foods that mirror what the family is eating. Another good practice is to offer vegetables at the beginning of meals, before offering other foods such as meats, grains, or fruits. Studies show that children consume significantly more vegetables in the first year of life if they were weaned first with vegetables as opposed to fruits.

The texture of food also matters in building acceptance. Offering the same foods in a variety of different textures, for example, puréed, roughly mashed, or as larger-sized finger foods (as age appropriate), is correlated with greater acceptance of that particular food, as well as with lower fussiness overall. Again, introduce texture early. Studies show that children who were exposed to more roughly textured food (i.e., purées with some lumps) at around six months showed much less picky eating than those exposed to these textures after nine months.

Third, expose children to the same foods frequently and repeatedly. Researchers agree that as many as ten to fifteen exposures might be needed to get a child to accept a particular food. This is especially true of vegetables because of the bitter flavor. It usually takes more tries to get kids to like new vegetables than to like new fruits. Unfortunately, studies also show that most parents give up and decide that their child doesn't like a food after only five tries. The lesson is keep trying!

A final rule is to follow your baby's lead. Let your child eat at her own pace and self-adjust intake. It is important that children tap into the satiety cues of their own bodies. In this way, they learn to stop eating when they're full, which promotes better appetite control and a healthy weight later on in life.

SCHOOL-AGE KIDS

Once kids are in their school-age years (roughly, five to eleven years old), it can feel as if their dislike for certain foods is set in stone, and it's easy for you to give up on a wide range of foods that your child has put in the "I'll never eat that!" category. But research shows that at this age children's tastes are still very malleable. This section will address how to reintroduce foods that kids say they expressly dislike, as well as to continue introducing new foods and flavors at this age.

Believe it or not, the most reliable strategy for getting kids at this age to like a previously disliked food is still repeated exposure. Studies show that as little as three to eight positive new experiences with a food kids say they don't like can get them to change their minds. And, just as with babies, exposures do not require that children eat a large amount of the food, just that they take small tastes. That said, "exposure" at this age is not as simple as putting some bits of steamed spinach or mashed sweet potato in front of them as you can do with babies. At this stage, you have to get a bit more sophisticated!

Let's step back a minute and think about the developmental stage of school-age children. They are curious and energetic. They're learning to read and write, making friends, and developing their own unique topics of interest. To encourage healthy eating at this age, it's important to tie food to their sense of exploration, their sponge-like capacity to learn, and their friendships.

One technique for overcoming dislike is something researchers call "associative conditioning." This means pairing a food that kids say they don't like with something they do like and view positively. This positive thing could be a different food they do enjoy. For example, you may pair broccoli florets with a dip you know they like (like the Healthy Ranch Dressing in Chapter 6), or mix it into a recipe they otherwise enjoy, like a pasta dish (see Pesto Pasta in Chapter 8). In this way, you condition them to associate broccoli with other foods they like, and it reduces the negative opinion they had of this vegetable. This is simple and it *works*—many studies support this approach.

The positive associative experience can also be nonfood related. For example, as a lead-up to introducing a new food, you can read a book about the cuisine, culture, and geography of a particular food. There are many such books—lean on them to build anticipation and excitement! You could also pair foods with an activity kids enjoy, like serving healthy snacks after a baseball game or on a special family picnic. You should note that pairing healthy foods with rewards such as access to a particular toy or to unhealthy foods (dessert) has *not* been shown to work and may backfire over time. Neither of these methods overcomes the negativity bias kids have toward the food; it just creates a temporary incentive. In the case of dessert, it may even reinforce their negative feelings toward the healthier foods.

School-age children often eat away from home, including at school, friends' houses, and sports events, and they are increasingly influenced by what their peers eat. As your children grow, you can't control every food interaction they have, and that's okay. It's important to remember that, regardless of what they encounter outside the home, the food environment you create in your home makes a big and lasting impact. The most important consideration is that the food environment you can control should be one of fun, inclusiveness, and experimentation, rather than one of worry, stress, and punishment.

TEENS

Teenage years are a chance for kids to develop independence and prepare for adulthood, within the safety net of family support. With this incremental independence also comes greater self-expression. Teens may put together their own outfits (often over the cringes of parents), decorate their bedrooms, and choose whom they hang out with. They have a say in these matters, but within limits (no wearing ripped jeans to a fancy wedding!). And so it goes with food. You want your teens to become their own people, try new things, and have new experiences, but you want them to be safe doing it. Trying vegetarianism in an omnivorous household? Great! Having a favorite candy and overindulging occasionally? It comes with the age. Eating only ultra-processed food? Skipping meals because your teen feels too fat? These will require thoughtful parent intervention.

It's a mistake to think of the teenage years only through the lens of rebellion. They may equally be one of curiosity and increasing sophistication when it comes to food. This is a time when kids are fully coming into their "food voice," a term coined by author and nutritionist Annie Hauck, which means that what you choose to eat can make a powerful statement about who you are or want to be. Physiologically, it is also a time when palates are more open to a wide variety of flavors. Notably, the preference for bitter tastes *increases* in early adolescence, which means a wider variety of vegetables, nuts, seeds, herbs, and spices may be on the table. Help teens grow their food voice and new openness by introducing them to cuisines from around the world, at home, through cookbooks and media, in restaurants, and with their peers (who are increasingly influential to food choice during adolescence). Finally, this is an important time for kids to build the skills they will need to eventually nourish themselves healthfully. Encourage them to take some responsibility for choosing what's for dinner—and also for doing some of the work that goes into meal planning, budgeting, shopping, cooking, and cleaning up.

MITIGATING ALLERGIES THROUGH EARLY EXPOSURE

Perhaps you have noticed and wondered about the rise in number of children with food allergies, or maybe someone in your family or community is affected by them. Although research is very active in this important area, scientific consensus is currently lacking on definitive reasons for this change. Researchers have gained some insight into approaches to help mitigate the risk of allergy development. The key is early introduction to possible allergens in small doses so that the body learns to treat these foods as friend, not foe. This is a significant reversal of earlier recommendations and is driven by the surprising findings of several landmark studies.

In 2015, the LEAP study (Learning Early about Peanut Allergy) showed that children who were introduced to peanuts between four and eleven months had substantially lower incidence of peanut allergies at age five than a control group that abstained from peanut introduction. A subsequent study in 2016 called EAT (Enquiring About Tolerance) confirmed these findings with a longer list of potential allergens, including egg, cow's milk, sesame, whitefish, and wheat. Additional studies have shown that early exposure to potential allergens such as wheat and eggs may be associated with lower prevalence later in life of asthma and eczema. Indeed, one study showed that higher maternal intake of peanuts, milk, and wheat during early pregnancy was associated with reduced odds of mid-childhood allergy and asthma.

In sum, it appears that there is a critical window between four and six months during which immune tolerance is achieved. This means that during this time, in many children, exposures to very small amounts of potentially allergenic foods will allow them to develop tolerance to the food. The best and safest way to do this is to treat these foods much as you would any other—introduce very small amounts, for example a drop on the outer lip or tongue, and observe children's reaction. In the case of peanuts and tree nuts, it is recommended to introduce them in powder or flour form. Peanut powder is readily available, and you can find many other nuts and seeds in flour form, including almond, hazelnut, sunflower seeds, and more. Simply dilute a very small amount of nut powder or flour in applesauce or another purée. You may also dilute *smooth* nut or seed butters in water or applesauce. *Do not* give your infant non–diluted nut butters, whole nuts, or crushed nuts, as these are a choking hazard. Work with your child's doctor to determine the time frame and pace best suited to your child.

Important note: If your baby is at high risk for peanut allergies (primary risk factors include family history, severe eczema, and egg allergy), it is critically important that you talk with your pediatrician *before* introducing peanuts and any tree nuts so you can make a safe plan together.

MODELING HEALTHY AND ADVENTUROUS EATING

Finally, while exposure is key to introducing your child to new foods, he will decide what is good to eat not only based on his taste buds, but also on his observation of what others around him are eating. This is what researchers call "modeling." Babies and young children are especially sensitive to the food behaviors that their primary caretakers model. You can offer your baby butternut squash over and over again, but if she sees that you're not eating it, she's less likely to eat it herself. Children see through this and emulate what you *do* rather than what you *say*. We know this instinctively when we enthusiastically mime eating baby food to get infants to eat. But it is not so different for older kids. Vegetables need to be part of the aromas in the kitchen and welcomed guests at the table for kids of all ages to accept vegetables. This is not just folk wisdom; it is also upheld by scientific study.

In order for modeling to work, your child's food should "match" the rest of the family's meals as early and as often as possible. That's why, in this book, we have chosen not to create separate sections for baby food, foods for toddlers, and so on. Instead, we encourage you to think of each recipe as one that can work for the whole family, with a little tweaking to make it appropriate for children at different stages of life. For babies, this means pulling out a few ingredients from recipes that can be mashed or cut into finger foods. For toddlers, this can mean serving the same components of the rest of the family's meal, with a bit less salt and spices, and presented more simply on their plates. For example, the components of the Breakfast Tostadas (see Chapter 7) can be served on a plate as separate finger foods—eggs, bean dip, avocado, and Pico de Gallo (see Chapter 11)—rather than piled onto a tortilla.

In the US, the food industry spends millions each year seeking to convince parents that "kids' food" is a completely separate category from adult food and that parents should therefore buy "kid-friendly" products (which are largely processed). We encourage you to throw the idea of kids' food out the window. It's a marketing strategy without basis in science. In fact, studies show that eating ready-prepared food contributes to pickiness. In contrast, in many cultures around the world, kids eat the same things as the rest of the family, just modified to meet their developmental needs. Food for children doesn't need to be overly sweet or packaged into a funny shape. It should be just as vibrant and full of interesting spices as adult food. In fact, that's exactly how children learn to eat like adults.

You may ask, "What about baby food?" Overall, if chosen thoughtfully, there's nothing wrong with buying prepared baby food for some meals. Jarred baby food certainly has some advantages—it's easy to stock in your pantry or to bring on a trip, and of course it takes no prep work. Many regularly available brands of baby food have just a few whole-foods ingredients, and an increasing number of brands offer organic options, which is important because pesticides have been found to make their way into baby food. The best way to determine quality is to read the ingredients list. Choose only baby food without any artificial coloring and chemical additives. Plastic packaging can also impart unwanted chemicals. It is best to buy it in glass jars.

However, even high-quality jarred baby food has several major disadvantages. First, it misses an opportunity to integrate your baby into the family's meals and expose her to the food diversity of *your* particular household. When your baby eats food that resembles what the rest of the family eats, she learns to match her observations from other senses—smelling what's cooking in the kitchen, watching what's served to siblings—with her own experience of food. A further disadvantage of jarred baby food is that it needs to be heated to very high temperatures and/or preserved with citric acid to keep safely at room temperature. This compromises both taste and nutrient value (some vitamins are lost through heat). Compare the flavor of a mashed fresh banana to jarred banana purée and you'll quickly see how muted the jarred one is. Baby food manufacturers also tend to mix sweet ingredients, such as fruits, into every formula to make them more palatable. This misses the opportunity to get your baby used to the nuanced, complex flavors of non-sweet foods, in particular dark green vegetables (which are almost never a lead ingredient in jarred baby food). Finally, store-bought baby food tends to be a uniformly smooth texture, which doesn't allow for the early introduction of more complex textures and can lead to more picky eating. These uniform and muted flavors do little to prepare your baby for the complexity of real foods and can make transition to table foods more difficult. Best practices for feeding babies is to offer them foods from the family's table early and often. Making baby food yourself can be as easy as roughly mashing some steamed broccoli, a baked sweet potato, or cooked beans; it doesn't have to be inconvenient or complicated, and you will save money in the process.

Finally, eating as a family in this united way has one more added benefit: It means that parents do not turn into short-order cooks! You do not need to make one meal for your toddler, another for your teen, and a third for adults in the house. It's a waste of your time and counterproductive when it comes to teaching children to eat healthfully.

SUMMARY: TIPS FOR EXPANDING YOUR CHILD'S PALATE

- Provide repeated exposure to new foods, especially to a variety of vegetables. Remember that ten to fifteen positive experiences may be needed.
- Introduce a variety of flavors and textures early (including in utero).

- Cultivate a culture of "adventurous eating" in your family by reading books about world cuisines and exploring foods from many different cultures at home and in restaurants.
- Kids and adults eat together. Adults model good eating habits, and children are offered the same food as adults, modified for their developmental stage. Parents are not short-order cooks!
- As kids increase their independence, give them a greater say in (and responsibility for) family meals.
- Don't give up! Expect refusal and try not to get overly anxious about it. Stay consistent and focus on long-term goals, which is to educate your child about how to be a healthy and adventurous eater for life.

CHAPTER 4

Making Mealtime Happy and Healthy

There is a lot of attention in the media on *what* we eat, and less on *how*. But the context of eating is a key part of the anti-inflammatory way. Positive food environments not only make it easy to choose healthy foods; they also help to combat the stress of everyday life, which is itself a major cause of inflammation.

EAT TOGETHER AS A FAMILY

The first step to creating a positive food culture in your home is to eat together as a family when possible. This simple act has impressive potential benefits across nutrition, child development, and family dynamics. Increased frequency of family dinners has been correlated with greater academic achievement and vocabulary growth in children; increased fruit and vegetable consumption; overall better nutrition; and reduced risk of substance abuse, obesity, and eating disorders in teens. Eating together also creates opportunities for modeling positive eating behaviors and normalizing eating foods that might be new to children, both of which are critically important factors in raising healthy and adventurous eaters.

The feeling and context of mealtimes are just as important as frequency. Studies show that the benefits of eating together are most pronounced when the social atmosphere during meals is positive. Social meals encourage children to try new foods with greater ease and less stress. While each family's culture is unique, researchers define a positive social atmosphere as one in which parents are engaged and responsive to children's questions, communicate in a clear and direct manner, and create a sense of order and structure around mealtimes. You can reinforce this by setting expectations that everyone comes to the table at the same time; shuts off ringers, screens, and other electronics; engages in conversation; and pitches in to set the table and clean up.

ENCOURAGE MINDFUL (AND SCREEN-FREE) EATING

Mindfulness is a practice of paying close attention to what's happening in your body and mind moment to moment. It is based on Buddhist meditation practices and has been translated into secular form by many Westerners. It has been shown to be effective in helping people reduce the stress of modern living, in addition to helping to alleviate pain, anxiety, and depression. Mindful eating is paying close attention while you eat. This is a very rich area of practice and research, and we can't do justice to the breadth of it here, but we will highlight some of the benefits of mindful eating because of how powerful it can be as part of the anti-inflammatory way.

There isn't one perfect way to do mindful eating. It is one part attitude and one part practice. The attitude you want to cultivate is kindness and non-judgment. This means, for example, that while it's important to choose healthy foods most of the time, when you (or your children) enjoy treats, throw out the inner critic and thoroughly enjoy them. The practice part can take many forms, but usually involves the following:

- Savoring your food slowly, including taking small bites and chewing thoroughly (like twenty to forty times, which will seem like a lot, but you may be surprised by how interesting it is to watch the flavor and texture change)
- Paying close attention to the effect of food on your senses (how it smells, feels on your tongue, sounds, and so on)
- Noting any sensations or emotions that come up, including feelings of hunger and satiety
- Eating free of distractions (especially screen-free!) or even observing silence

Now, asking your children to observe whole meals in silence and chew their every bite thirty times is not a prescription we're offering. Very rigid mindfulness practices can actually conflict with the benefits of social eating previously mentioned. Explore ways to blend mindful and social eating that work for your family. For example, you may want to start meals by bringing awareness and gratitude to all that went into making them, from the sun, plants, and farmers, to the hands that cooked the meal. You can do a once-per-meal slow-chewing activity, where family members share what they observed. You can encourage your children (and yourself) to tap into your hunger and satiety cues by asking questions that focus attention on these feelings at different points in the meal: "Are you super hungry? A little hungry? How full do you feel?" And even observing a couple of minutes of collective silent eating is very powerful!

Mindful eating has been shown to be effective in bringing awareness to food choices, helping you tap into your satiety cues, and reducing emotional and binge eating. Conversely, watching TV or engaging with other screens during meals is associated with negative health outcomes, including reduced intake of fruits and vegetables, higher rates of obesity, and decreased attention to satiety cues, leading both children and adults to overeat. Of course, focusing attention on screens reduces both social eating and mindful eating and the many positive benefits that come with them. In short, make the dining table a phone-, TV-, and screen-free zone. Pay attention to the food, your own sensations, and to one another. These practices can form the basis for a lifetime of healthy, attuned eating.

ENCOURAGE DESCRIPTIVE FOOD LANGUAGE

One great way to practice mindfulness is through the language you choose. We strongly suggest establishing a dining table culture whose language is respectful and curious. Discourage black-and-white terms like "good/bad," "yum/yuck," or "like/don't like" to describe foods, as well as the use of very negative words like "gross" or "hate." Instead, encourage the whole family, children and adults alike, to use words that are descriptive. Ask your child to describe the color, texture, smell, and flavor of foods. They may use words like "crunchy," "squishy," "sweet," "tingles on my tongue," or they may have more playful descriptions like "it reminds me of the smell of grass." You can make a game of this at mealtimes— see how many words each person can come up with! One brilliant cooking teacher we've worked with encouraged kids to use the word "interesting" at first if they were unsure about a food. Kids made a big game of this and took to rubbing their chins like curious scientists, saying, "Ah yes, this apricot is very *interesting*," and then erupting into giggles about how sour it was in their mouths. Also, encourage respect for individual preferences and discourage groupthink. A younger sibling who idolizes an older one may be easily swayed ("Yeah, I think peas are gross too!"). There is nothing wrong with disliking a food, but encourage children to think for themselves and articulate what features of the food are not to their liking. And ask that older siblings keep their negative opinions of food to themselves!

One wonderful activity for teaching children to recognize and embrace new flavors and textures is the taste-test activity (see Chapter 5). This activity is based on many workshops we have done with children over the years. It is also similar to activities that researchers have conducted in schools with children of all ages, which have consistently shown that small exposures such as those in this tasting activity can lead to greater openness to a wider variety of foods. Try it at home with the whole family!

MAKE THE HEALTHY CHOICE THE EASY CHOICE

The food environment in the US today is not an easy one in which to raise healthy eaters. A short list of the multibillion-dollar marketing campaigns food companies use to sell junk food includes distribution on TV commercials; Internet sites and ads on social media; product placement in movies; athlete, celebrity, or cartoon endorsements; placing sugary cereals and junk foods at kids' eye level in supermarkets...and there are many more. All these techniques are designed to promote the "nag factor," the tendency of children to relentlessly nag their parents for heavily advertised, ultra-processed food, until parents succumb in desperation to stop the nagging. This uneven playing field is one that many are fighting to fix by advocating for more stringent regulations with regard to advertising food to children (following the example of restricting tobacco ads to kids).

What can you do to combat the aggressive junk food marketing industry? Limiting exposure to commercials and advertisements is a first line of defense. When nagging does occur, effective techniques include remaining calm, but firm and consistent, rather than arguing with your child; setting rules and expectations before leaving the house for shopping trips; and redirecting them to choose a healthier treat they want instead of the junk food.

Also know that children's food habits are established in the home, and focus on making your home environment one that encourages healthy choices. There is a growing field called "food choice architecture," which shows that the environmental context or "architecture" in which food is presented deeply influences the food choices you make.

You can use this approach to nudge, rather than nag, children and adults toward choosing anti-inflammatory foods by adopting some of the tactics of the food industry itself. For example, where food is placed and what kind of container it's in matters. Put already-cut fruits and vegetables in a clear container at the front of the refrigerator. Place healthy snacks at eye level and arm's reach for both kids and adults. Conversely, put cookies and other occasional treats in opaque containers and in less-easy-to-reach places. You can also engage in your own marketing strategies, like "VIP endorsements"—your child may have a favorite stuffed animal that suddenly develops a love for peas, or a beloved uncle who joins you for dinner and sings the praises of broccoli. Stickers can be surprisingly effective. In one study, smiley face stickers and "good for you!" signs attached to fruits and vegetables in a school cafeteria encouraged students to eat more of these foods—and this was with adolescents! And, when serving foods, plate size matters. Larger plates will encourage eating larger portions. If you are worried about your child's weight, or your own, consider the size of your dishes and serving utensils. Consider these ideas and apply the lens of food choice architecture—is your kitchen designed to make the healthy choice the *easy choice*?

AVOID FOOD BATTLES

Finally, avoid food battles. There is a fine line between repeatedly encouraging children to try food and pressuring them. This is an important line for parents to find and understand. Studies show that cajoling or arguing with children about food, appearing overly worried, being too prescriptive, or using food as reward or punishment can all backfire. It may create greater psychological resistance on the part of your child, which has little to do with the food itself, but is instead about asserting autonomy. If you find yourself in this trap, shift your focus off your child's every bite to creating a social, mindful, and relaxed mealtime environment. Remember that your consistent modeling of healthy eating is very influential in the long run, where it matters.

Limit Snacking

One great way to avoid food battles is to make sure kids are hungry at mealtime. Limiting snacks and caloric drinks between meals increases children's appetite during main meals. Kids in the US today receive around three snacks per day, which is a major increase from the 1970s, when it was closer to once per day. Snacks seem to find their way into every event, from sports to school to car rides to strolls in the park. Further, a majority of calories kids get from snacks tend to be low quality, especially high in sugar, refined carbohydrates, and salt. When you do offer snacks, make them healthy ones like those presented in this book, which are rich in plant foods and protein. Even then, put overall limits on in-between meal noshing. Experts agree that this will encourage children to try more new foods at main meals.

COOK TOGETHER!

Our most enthusiastic suggestion is this final one: cook together! Similar to eating as a family, cooking together has impressive benefits. Numerous studies, in addition to our collective decades of empirical evidence, show that involving children in hands-on cooking activities makes them much more willing to try new foods and, in particular, to eat more fruits and vegetables. We can't count the times a child who professes to dislike broccoli suddenly forgets this fact when she makes a broccoli quesadilla with her own hands. Simply put, children eat more food when they prepare it themselves. Cooking creates a sense of empowerment and pride and helps to overcome neophobia. This extends as well to precooking activities such as meal planning and shopping. Getting kids' input from the start about the week's meals, and the intended shopping list, builds in a sense of ownership and acceptance right from the start (and helps curtail the nag factor fights).

We know that when you're feeling hurried, the idea of involving children in making dinner can feel like an added burden. Kids take longer with the tasks, need supervision, and may be clumsy at first. But as their skills improve, even young children can be genuinely helpful in the kitchen. They can tear lettuce leaves for salad; pinch herbs (remove the leaves from the stems); mix, knead, spread, or grate cheese or vegetables (with supervision to safeguard knuckles); and even quite young children can safely use plastic knives to cut soft foods like tofu, cheeses, and many fruits and vegetables. Solicit children's input in seasoning—does this need a bit more salt or some lemon? You can also ask them to "decorate" the meal with fruits, herbs, or vegetables before serving. These tactics might slow you down or make for a messier kitchen—try to let go in order to reap the rewards at the table.

Remember to start small. Give children one task to complete for each meal until they gain some proficiency, and then layer on more. Always demonstrate tasks, and always supervise for safety. For example, if you need Cheddar cheese cut in half-inch cubes, put a sample of a cube at the top of their cutting board so they can continually refer to it. Also, start young. We've cooked with groups of children as young as two years old, and they love it. By the time they're teens, they should be able to cook for *you*! In fact, one of the greatest benefits in cooking programs we've run with teens was the pride and empowerment they felt in their new ability to prepare family meals with confidence. So, if your teen complains about your dinner menu, you can counter with an invitation for them to prepare a meal they would prefer for the entire family.

In addition to including children in regular meal preparation, set aside time for special cooking activities, alone with your child or with small groups of kids. Recipes with the "CT" (Cook Together) tag lend themselves especially well to this. And don't underestimate the fun of making a simple fruit, yogurt, and granola parfait. For pointers on safely cooking with children of all ages, see Tips for Cooking with Kids in Chapter 5.

SUMMARY: TIPS FOR MAKING MEALTIMES HAPPY AND HEALTHY

- Cultivate a mealtime environment that is social, relaxed, and screen-free. Put away the phones and tablets, turn off the TV, and talk to one another.
- Encourage everyone in the family to eat slowly, mindfully, and tap into their own satiation cues. It's okay to stop eating when you feel full.
- Encourage descriptive language. Something being yummy or gross is not enough—what is it about the food that you like or find unappealing?
- Use smart food choice architecture to make the healthy choice easy to find and desirable in your home.
- Avoid negativity and pressure/cajoling. Food is neither a reward nor a punishment.
- Limit snacking in between meals so children are hungry for main meals, which tend to be more nutritious.
- Include children in hands-on cooking. They are *much* more adventurous eaters when they are involved in making meals!

CHAPTER 5

A Guide to Recipes and Cooking with Kids

This chapter provides a guide to our recipes, including understanding recipe tags, making substitutions, and accommodating allergies. You'll also find a weekly sample menu, tips for how to get your kids safely involved in the kitchen, and a fun taste-test activity.

RECIPE TAGS

You will notice recipe tags on each of the recipes in this book. Here's what they mean:

- GF **Gluten-free:** The recipe contains no wheat or gluten.
- DF **Dairy-free:** This recipe contains no dairy.
- EF **Egg-free:** This recipe contains no eggs.
- NF **Nut-free:** This recipe contains no peanuts or tree nuts.
- CT **Cook Together:** This is a recipe that makes an especially good hands-on cooking activity with kids, either at home when time allows, or at a special event like a birthday party.

REMOVING ALLERGENS

Note that many of the recipes that do have gluten, dairy, eggs, or nuts can easily be converted to allergen-free. We give specific guidance in the recipe headnotes on how you may do this. Don't consider any recipe off-limits until you look at these notes! Here are some general guidelines:

- **To convert to gluten-free:** Substitute gluten-free pasta, bread, or flour for wheat-based products.
- **To convert to dairy-free:** Substitute coconut oil for butter (1:1), use an alternative milk, and/or remove the small amount of dairy without any negative impact on taste.
- **To convert to egg-free:** In many of our baked recipes and batters, you may substitute Flax Eggs (see recipe in Chapter 6).

SUBSTITUTIONS

Recipes are not technical manuals for assembling precision electronics. Rather, think of a recipe as a guide and an invitation to use your creativity and judgment. If you ask us about a substitution, omission, replacement, or other variations, the answer is almost always, "Sure!" Can I leave out the red pepper? Can I double the garlic? Can I use oil instead of butter? Can I double the batch and have leftovers? "Sure!"

If you are a novice cook, you will be pleased to find most of our recipes are detailed and simple to follow. Following the instructions closely will give you the confidence to know you are on the right track, making the recipes as they were done in our kitchens. If you are a comfortable and experienced cook, use the recipes for inspiration and vary them according to the tastes of your family and ingredient availability. Don't just follow recipes—invent them!

Here are some easy substitutions:

- **Nuts and seeds:** They are mostly interchangeable in our recipes. Use walnuts if you don't have hazelnuts, or swap sunflower seeds for pumpkin seeds. The same holds true of dried fruit—we include some fancier ingredients like dried blueberries or cherries, but raisins are just as good and more cost-conscious!
- **Greens:** Kale, collards, Swiss chard, mustards, spinach, bok choy...they're mostly interchangeable, with different cooking times.
- **Cheeses:** Hard grating cheeses like Parmigiano and pecorino are interchangeable, as are melting cheeses like Cheddar and Swiss.
- **Spices:** We love our homemade anti-inflammatory spice blends. But if you're in a pinch, simple cinnamon and cardamom work in place of the Sweet Spice Blend. Our Basic Anti-Inflammatory Spice Blend is somewhat similar to curry blends, and the Tex-Mex Spice Blend can be swapped for chili powder.

DON'T WORRY ABOUT PERFECT

With the recipes in this book, don't worry too much about precision. As long as knife cuts are relatively uniform so things cook evenly, they don't need to be perfect or pretty. A general rule is as follows:

- Small dice = about ¼"
- Medium dice = about ½"
- Large dice = about 1"

BABY FOOD

In many cultures, "baby food" doesn't exist. It's just called food, portioned and mashed appropriately for the youngest eaters. One of the best ways to avoid picky eaters and introduce a wide variety of foods to babies is to match their food with the rest of the family's food early. For nearly every recipe in this book, we give instructions for how to make it safe and appropriate for babies. Most desserts do not have recommendations for baby food alternatives because it is recommended that children under two years old consume no added sugar. A mashed banana, unsweetened applesauce, or nearly any fruit purée is plenty sweet for babies. Similarly, the beverages that include juice are not recommended for babies.

WEEKLY MENU SAMPLE

While making multiple meals each week may seem daunting, a little planning can reduce time and effort. By over-preparing and incorporating leftovers, one meal can flow from the other. Here is a sample menu for a week:

Sunday

- **Hearty brunch:** Breakfast Tostadas (Chapter 7) (make 2 × Pinto Bean Dip recipe [Chapter 11]; blend only half and store the other half in refrigerator)
- **Snack (and kids' cooking project):** Banana Quinoa Muffins (Chapter 7) (make and refrigerate extra quinoa) and Strawberry "Milk" (Chapter 13)
- **Dinner:** Meatball and Escarole Soup (Chapter 9) (eat half, put leftover in refrigerator) served with toasted whole-wheat bread drizzled with olive oil and Dukkah (Chapter 6)
- **Prep for the week:** Make one batch of Amaranth-Millet Porridge (Chapter 7); bake a few whole sweet potatoes and make one batch of roasted sweet potatoes for the Quinoa and Sweet Potato Bowls with Avocado Dressing (Chapter 8)

Monday

- **Breakfast:** Warm Amaranth-Millet Porridge (Chapter 7) with Sweet Spiced Ghee (Chapter 6), top with fresh fruit and yogurt (using precooked porridge)

- **Lunch:** Quinoa and Sweet Potato Bowls with Avocado Dressing (Chapter 8) (using precooked quinoa and sweet potatoes)
- **Dinner:** Fish Tacos (Chapter 9) with Fennel Slaw (Chapter 10) and (leftover) Pinto Bean Dip (Chapter 11). Serve with Pico de Gallo (make 2 × recipe) (Chapter 11)

Tuesday

- **Breakfast:** Banana Quinoa Muffins (Chapter 7) (leftover muffins) with Golden Milk Smoothie (Chapter 13)
- **Lunch:** Green 'n' Beans Quesadillas (Chapter 8) with (leftover) Pico de Gallo (Chapter 11)
- **Dinner:** Meatball and Escarole Soup (Chapter 9) (from leftovers), stretched with small pasta shells or rice

Wednesday

- **Breakfast:** Turmeric Scrambled Eggs (Chapter 7) with Sweet Potato Silver Dollars (sweet potatoes already baked) (Chapter 7)
- **Lunch:** Tempeh Sticks with Cilantro Dip (Chapter 8)
- **Dinner:** Nut-Coated Chicken Tenders (make 2 × recipe) (Chapter 8) with Coconut Kale (Chapter 10)

Thursday

- **Breakfast:** Warm Amaranth-Millet Porridge (Chapter 7) (using precooked porridge) with Sweet Spiced Ghee (Chapter 6), topped with fresh fruit and yogurt
- **Lunch:** Nut-Coated Chicken Tenders (leftover) (Chapter 8) in a sandwich, with vegetable sticks and Healthy Ranch Dressing (Chapter 6) (store remaining dressing in refrigerator)
- **Dinner:** Eggplant Shakshuka (Chapter 9) and side salad with Lemon-Tahini Dressing (Chapter 6) (store remaining dressing in refrigerator)

Friday

- **Breakfast:** Tofu Scramble (Chapter 7) with Sweet Potato Silver Dollars (sweet potatoes from leftovers) (Chapter 7)
- **Lunch:** Mackerel Salad Sandwich (Chapter 8) with vegetable sticks and (leftover) Healthy Ranch Dressing (Chapter 6)
- **Dinner:** Vegetable Pita Pizzas (Chapter 8) and mixed green salad with (leftover) Lemon-Tahini Dressing (Chapter 6)
- **Dessert:** Dark Chocolate Bark (Chapter 12) or Spiced Chocolate Fondue with Fruit Kebabs (Chapter 12)

Saturday

- **Breakfast:** Buckwheat-Applesauce Pancakes (Chapter 7) with Tahini Maple Syrup (Chapter 6)
- **Lunch:** Swiss Chard and Feta Frittata (Chapter 8) (store leftovers for Monday lunch)
- **Snack (and cooking activity with kids):** Blueberry-Hazelnut Bars (Chapter 11)
- **Dinner:** Try a new restaurant!

TIPS FOR COOKING WITH KIDS

Cooking with kids should be fun and not overly full of rules. But instilling good kitchen practices from a young age will make the process smoother, safer, and more rewarding. Here are our best tips for cooking with your kids, culled from many years of teaching cooking to kids of all ages.

- **Start with sanitation:** Have kids wash their hands thoroughly before handling food and in between tasks (especially if they touch raw meat, fish, or eggs). Emphasize and model having a clean "working station"—do one thing at a time and tidy up in between.
- **Practice safe knife skills:** Children should only use knives with proper knife technique and close adult supervision. Tailor the type of knife and cutting task to your child's age and skill level. For example, small plastic knives and

soft ingredients are safer for young cooks, while adolescents may be able to handle small chef's knives. Also teach proper knife handling. There are many good resources on the Internet, including illustrations and videos of the following hand position. Watch and practice these with your child, and start each cooking activity with a quick review of knife safety.

- The hand that holds the knife should always "choke up" on the knife, holding it near the blade rather than from the far end. This gives the most control. The other hand should be in the chef's "claw" formation—fingers curled under; thumb tucked in the back of your three middle fingers. In this way, your knuckles safely guide the knife blade, and fingertips are out of harm's way.

- **Emphasize overall kitchen safety:** Beyond knife use, point out other kitchen hazards, including hot stoves and pans, and potentially dangerous appliances. Remember that things you take for granted (one should not practice pirouettes near the stove) may not be obvious to an energetic child.

- **Show, don't tell:** Show kids what to do and demonstrate how to do it. Let go of perfectionism and the urge to do it for them. This is all about a hands-on experience.

- **Encourage frequent tasting:** Ask kids to sample each ingredient they handle and ask their opinion on seasonings as the food cooks. Encourage descriptive language, beyond "good" or "yuck"—is it crunchy, sour, tingly, grassy?

- **Engage curiosity:** Encourage kids to use all their senses to observe the smell, texture, color, taste, and even sound of the food. Engage their curiosity about the natural world by asking them questions. "What do you think will happen to the eggs when we heat them in the pan?" "How long do you think the cookies will take to bake? Let's time it and see if we're right."

- **Start small:** There is no need for kids to help in every step of the process—and often plenty of reasons for them not to. For most meals, find some small, manageable tasks that kids might enjoy, like filling muffin tins, chopping a single ingredient, plucking herbs, or even decorating a plate. This will help build skills gradually.

- **Relax:** Apart from safety concerns, where you should be vigilant, the biggest risk of having kids cook may be a messy countertop or kitchen floor. Let it happen...and get them to help clean up after!

TASTE TEST

This taste-test activity's goal is to encourage kids and adults alike to appreciate the nuances of foods and to use descriptive language. This helps move beyond black-and-white thinking about food (good/bad, I like/don't like).

Scientifically speaking, what we commonly refer to as our sense of "taste" is actually a multisensory experience that involves three senses—taste, smell, and touch—which combine to create a holistic perception that is more accurately called *flavor*. To date, scientists have identified five tastes that we can detect with our tongues: sweet, salty, sour, bitter, and umami. Heat, or spiciness, is processed not through taste buds but through pain fibers called nociceptors. In other words, it is perceived through touch rather than taste, as are many other qualities of food, such as the mouthfeel of fat or the crunch of a chip. Finally, smell is the most nuanced of the three senses. Our noses can detect millions of unique smells! Thus taste, touch, and smell combine to give us the capacity to perceive an untold variety of complex flavors.

To prepare for this taste test, choose ingredients that represent all five tastes, plus heat, as well as various textures. Also choose foods that have complex flavors. For example, maple syrup is almost purely sweet. Cooked beets are also sweet, but they are earthy and a little bitter as well. Blueberries are sweet and tart at the same time. Likewise, whole foods often have multiple colors, textures, and aromas—encourage kids to name as many as they can. This makes the activity more interesting and builds an appreciation for the complexity of whole foods. When it comes to sensation, you can ask, "How does it feel in your mouth?" For example, a spicy food might tingle, a sour food will feel dry on the tongue, and an orange or cherry tomato explodes with juiciness.

Put a small amount of each ingredient into bowls—remember, it's just a taste! Give each participant a copy of the following chart and something to write with. Or, you can do the activity verbally.

Examples of Ingredients

- **Sweet:** Honey and maple syrup are very sweet; almost any fruit has more complex sweetness; vegetables such as carrots, beets, squash, and pumpkin.

- **Sour (aka tart or astringent):** Citrus, such as lemon, lime, grapefruit, and kumquat; many berries; fermented foods like yogurt and sauerkraut; spices like sumac; apple cider or balsamic vinegar.
- **Bitter:** Most greens, including lettuce leaves, baby kale, and herbs such as cilantro and basil (herbs have especially intense and complex flavors).
- **Salty:** Sea salt and soy sauce are obvious choices; miso; sea vegetables such as nori, dulse, or hijiki are great.
- **Umami (or savory):** Cooked shiitake mushrooms, miso, aged hard cheeses, and kombu (aka dried kelp—soften it in water to better taste it; kombu is how the umami taste was discovered and named in Japan in 1908!).
- **Hot/Spicy (sensation):** Ginger and garlic are great; horseradish (with caution); some chili powders, curry powders, and paprika; arugula and mustard greens.

NAME OF FOOD	COLORS	AROMAS	FLAVORS	SENSATIONS	TEXTURES

SUMMARY: TIPS FOR GETTING STARTED

- Don't sweat the small stuff. Imperfect knife cuts and substituted ingredients are welcomed—and encouraged. That's how you come up with something new and uniquely yours.
- Don't automatically pass on a recipe because it has an allergen you are avoiding. Chances are good that it's easy to take out—read recipe headnotes for guidance.
- Plan ahead so one meal's prep supports the next. Chop and cook more than you need; then use prepared ingredients and leftovers to save time.
- Invite kids to cook with you frequently. Teach them safety rules and demonstrate what to do. Then let go and trust them to learn.

CHAPTER 6

Anti-Inflammatory Spice Blends and Sauces

The anti-inflammatory spice blends and sauces in this chapter are the flavor (and health) foundation of most recipes in this book. The secret to making other meals fast and tasty is to invest 30 minutes once per week in making a few of these simple recipes. They take between 5–10 minutes each. You can use these blends for a variety of meals both in and beyond this book. You will quickly learn to rely on them, and then you may double or even triple the recipes. Spice blends can be stored in a glass jar for up to a year at room temperature.

You could also choose one to two sauces each week to make and then store them in the fridge. This way, you will always have a dressing for salads or a dip for vegetable sticks. Some are great drizzled on roasted vegetables, tofu or tempeh, chicken, or over pasta.

Finally, put spice blends on the table. There's no rule that says salt and pepper should be the only things to spice up your food. The Dukkah and Nori Gomasio are especially good table condiments.

Basic Anti-Inflammatory Spice Blend GF | DF | EF | NF | CT

This is a delicious combination of some of the most powerful anti-inflammatory spices nature provides. You can use it pretty much anywhere—as a seasoning on roasted vegetables, a rub for meat or fish, or as a flavor base for beans, grains, and soups.

Phytonutrient focus: Cumin, a core ingredient in this spice blend, has an impressive amount of research behind it, including on its heart-protective, anticancer, and antioxidant properties. It not only protects against inflammation, but may help to reduce high blood pressure too.

YIELDS 2½ TABLESPOONS | Prep Time: 5 minutes | Cook Time: n/a

2 teaspoons ground turmeric
2 teaspoons ground cumin
2 teaspoons ground coriander
½ teaspoon ground black pepper
½ teaspoon dry mustard powder
½ teaspoon ginger powder

Combine all ingredients in a glass jar. Mix well.

PER SERVING
(Serving size: 1 teaspoon)

Calories: 8 • Fat: 0g • Protein: 0g

Sodium: 2mg • Fiber: 1g

Carbohydrates: 1g • Net Carbs: 0g

Sugar: 0g

Savory Spiced Ghee   GF | EF | NF

Spiced ghee is useful as a base to cook eggs, to add to simple roasted vegetables, or to mix into mashed potatoes. It can be held at room temperature up to three months.

YIELDS ¼ CUP | Prep Time: 2 minutes | Cook Time: 5 minutes

¼ cup ghee

1 recipe (2½ tablespoons) Basic
   Anti-Inflammatory Spice
   Blend (see recipe in this
   chapter)

In a small saucepot over low heat, warm ghee until *just* melted (about 1–2 minutes). Add Basic Anti-Inflammatory Spice Blend, stir to combine, and turn off heat. Keep in a glass jar in the refrigerator until ready to use.

PER SERVING

(Serving size: 1 teaspoon)

Calories: 44 · Fat: 5g · Protein: 0g

Sodium: 1mg · Fiber: 0g

Carbohydrates: 1g · Net Carbs: 1g

Sugar: 0g

Sweet Spiced Ghee GF | EF | NF

Make a batch of this sweet ghee and keep it in a glass jar at room temperature up to three months. Use a spoonful on oatmeal, Amaranth-Millet Porridge (see Chapter 7), pancakes, or as a spread on toast.

Phytonutrient focus: A core spice in this blend is clove, whose potency is clear from its big, spicy taste. One of its main volatile oils, eugenol, has antibacterial, antioxidant, and anticancer properties. Clove is used in some toothpastes because it is effective against dental and gum diseases, which are indicators of systemic inflammation.

YIELDS 1 CUP | Prep Time: 5 minutes | Cook Time: 5 minutes

½ cup ghee
½ cup honey
1 recipe (2¼ tablespoons) Sweet Spice Blend (see recipe in this chapter)

1. Combine all ingredients in a small, heavy-bottomed pot.
2. Warm over very low heat until honey and ghee have *just* melted.
3. Store in a glass jar.

PER SERVING
(Serving size: 1 teaspoon)
Calories: 31 · Fat: 2g · Protein: 0g
Sodium: 0mg · Fiber: 0g
Carbohydrates: 3g · Net Carbs: 3g
Sugar: 3g

Sweet Spice Blend GF | DF | EF | NF | CT

This spice blend is a fantastic accompaniment to both sweet and savory foods. It is delicious mixed into granola or chocolate fondue, or used to make Sweet Spiced Delicata Squash (see Chapter 10). It can be hard to find star anise already ground, so grind it in a spice or coffee grinder—or leave it out, and it's still delicious!

Phytonutrient focus: Cardamom, a main ingredient in this spice blend, is a strongly aromatic herb with anti-inflammatory and antibacterial properties. Traditional wisdom holds that it improves digestion of other foods and treats digestive discomfort like bloating, nausea, or cramping (see herbal teas in Chapter 13). Best of all, it brings an uplifting, wonderful fragrance to many foods.

YIELDS 2¼ TABLESPOONS | Prep Time: 5 minutes | Cook Time: n/a

1 tablespoon ground cinnamon
1 tablespoon ground cardamom
½ teaspoon ground clove
½ teaspoon ground star anise

Combine all ingredients in a glass jar. Mix well.

PER SERVING
(Serving size: 1 teaspoon)

Calories: 6 · Fat: 0g

Protein: 0g · Sodium: 0mg

Fiber: 1g · Carbohydrates: 2g

Net Carbs: 1g · Sugar: 0g

Tex-Mex Spice Blend GF | DF | EF | NF | CT

This is a homemade version of chili powder. It's a simple, versatile, and tasty blend that is especially handy in spicing up beans, dips, and sauces.

Phytonutrient focus: Oregano is an excellent source of antioxidants with a high content of phenolic compounds. One of its volatile oils, thymol (which it shares with the herb thyme), is highly antimicrobial, helping to fight against bacteria and viruses. The best way to incorporate oregano is to use it frequently and in small doses.

YIELDS ¼ CUP | Prep Time: 5 minutes | Cook Time: n/a

1 tablespoon sweet paprika
1 tablespoon ground cumin
1 tablespoon dried oregano
1½ teaspoons red chili flakes
¾ teaspoon ground black pepper

In a glass jar, combine all the ingredients. Stir or shake well to mix.

PER SERVING

(Serving size: 1 teaspoon)

Calories: 5 · Fat: 0g

Protein: 0g · Sodium: 1mg

Fiber: 1g · Carbohydrates: 1g

Net Carbs: 0g · Sugar: 0g

Nori Gomasio GF | DF | EF | NF | CT

Gomasio is a sesame seed condiment found frequently on Japanese tables. Here, we add mineral and flavor-rich nori. Sprinkle this freely over rice, soups, salads, and stir-fries.

Phytonutrient focus: The tiny sesame seed is very versatile and used all over the world. It is made into condiments like this one; pressed into oil; and ground into tahini, which you'll find in many recipes in this book. It is highly antioxidant, due in part to its abundance of vitamin E and a group of phytochemicals called lignans, including a potent one named sesamol.

YIELDS ½ CUP | Prep Time: 10 minutes | Cook Time: n/a

1 sheet nori
½ cup sesame seeds
½ teaspoon salt

PER SERVING

(Serving size: 1 teaspoon)

Calories: 17 · Fat: 1g

Protein: 1g · Sodium: 48mg

Fiber: 0g · Carbohydrates: 1g

Net Carbs: 1g · Sugar: 0g

1. Holding nori with tongs, pass the sheet over a low-medium gas flame or electric burner on your stove quickly four times on each side. (Toasting nori this way makes it crisp and brings out its fragrance.)

2. Break nori apart with your fingers and put it in a spice or coffee grinder. Pulse a few times until nori is broken down into small flecks.

3. Add sesame seeds and pulse a few more times until seeds are roughly broken up.

4. Add salt, mix well, and keep in a glass jar at room temperature up to one month.

Avocado Dressing GF | DF | EF | NF | CT

This vibrant green dressing is made to please and full of healthy, anti-inflammatory fats. Its taste is most vibrant and fresh if eaten within about 24 hours from when it was made.

Phytonutrient focus: Avocados are a unique fruit. Instead of having a high sugar content, they are rich in fats. These are mostly monounsaturated fats, which have been associated with reducing cholesterol levels and the risk of cardiovascular disease. Avocados lend a silky texture to foods and make an excellent baby food. They are also high in vitamins E, B, and K.

YIELDS 1 CUP | Prep Time: 10 minutes | Cook Time: n/a

1 medium ripe avocado
¼ cup lime juice
2 cloves garlic, peeled
¼ cup packed fresh cilantro leaves
    and tender stems
¼ cup water
2 tablespoons extra-virgin olive
    oil
¼ teaspoon salt
¼ teaspoon ground black pepper

In a blender, combine all the ingredients. Blend until smooth. Serve.

PER SERVING

(Serving size: 1 tablespoon)

Calories: 30 · Fat: 3g

Protein: 0g · Sodium: 37mg

Fiber: 1g · Carbohydrates: 1g

Net Carbs: 0g · Sugar: 0g

Healthy Ranch Dressing GF | EF | NF | CT

Ranch is a favorite for salads and dipping vegetables. But store-bought ranch is usually made with unhealthy oils, unnecessary sugar, and a list of preservatives. This one is just real ingredients and tasty herbs and spices.

YIELDS 2 CUPS | Prep Time: 10 minutes | Cook Time: n/a

1 cup plain, whole milk Greek yogurt
½ cup buttermilk
¼ cup lemon juice
¼ cup chopped fresh dill
1 tablespoon fresh thyme leaves
1 teaspoon onion powder
1 teaspoon garlic powder
½ teaspoon ground black pepper
½ teaspoon salt

1. In a medium bowl, whisk together all ingredients.
2. Chill 30 minutes. Can keep in the refrigerator up to two weeks.

PER SERVING

(Serving size: 1 tablespoon)

Calories: 10 · Fat: 0g

Protein: 1g · Sodium: 42mg

Fiber: 0g · Carbohydrates: 1g

Net Carbs: 1g · Sugar: 1g

Walnut Pesto GF | EF | CT

Pesto is traditionally made with pine nuts, but here we use walnuts, which give a robust and earthy flavor. Remember to remove the hardest basil stems, but softer stems are okay to include.

Phytonutrient focus: Walnuts have been positively linked with brain health and cognitive performance, including a reduction of risk of Alzheimer's and other neurological diseases. They are excellent sources of omega-3 fatty acids, which also contribute to heart health and an overall decrease in inflammation.

YIELDS 1 CUP | Prep Time: 10 minutes | Cook Time: n/a

2 cups tightly packed fresh basil
¼ cup chopped walnuts
½ cup grated Parmigiano cheese
2 cloves garlic, peeled
½ cup extra-virgin olive oil
½ teaspoon salt
⅛ teaspoon ground black pepper

1. Combine all the ingredients in a food processor.
2. Process, stopping to scrape down the sides, until mixture is very smooth and well blended.
3. Taste and adjust seasoning. Keep in a sealed container in the refrigerator up to one week or frozen for six months.

PER SERVING

(Serving size: 1 tablespoon)

Calories: 85 · Fat: 8g

Protein: 1g · Sodium: 129mg

Fiber: 0g · Carbohydrates: 1g

Net Carbs: 1g · Sugar: 0g

Dukkah GF | DF | EF | CT

This Egyptian spice blend takes a bit more time than the other spice blends in this chapter because it involves roasting nuts and seeds for a few minutes. But it's *well* worth the time. Your family will fall in love with it! Sprinkle it on roasted vegetables, soups, salads, dips like hummus, or just on toasted bread with extra-virgin olive oil.

YIELDS 1 CUP | Prep Time: 10 minutes | Cook Time: 8 minutes

½ *cup whole hazelnuts*

2 tablespoons sunflower seeds

1 tablespoon cumin seeds

1 teaspoon fennel seeds

2½ tablespoons coriander seeds (or 1 tablespoon ground coriander powder)

2 tablespoons sesame seeds

½ *teaspoon nigella seeds*

1 teaspoon sweet paprika

½ *teaspoon salt*

¼ *teaspoon ground black pepper*

PER SERVING

(Serving size: 1 teaspoon)

Calories: 14 · Fat: 1g

Protein: 0g · Sodium: 24mg

Fiber: 0g · Carbohydrates: 1g

Net Carbs: 1g · Sugar: 0g

1. Preheat oven to 300°F.
2. Place hazelnuts and sunflower seeds on a sheet pan and toast about 5 minutes until fragrant.
3. Transfer to a spice grinder and pulse just until they are coarsely ground. (For this and other steps, a mortar and pestle could also be used.) Avoid getting to a flour stage; some pieces of nuts here and there are nice. Place in a small bowl.
4. Heat a small pan over medium heat for 1 minute. Then add cumin, fennel, and coriander (unless using already ground seeds). Toast 1 minute. Place in spice grinder and pulse until seeds are broken down but not powdered. Add spices to bowl with nuts.
5. In the same small pan, toast sesame seeds and nigella seeds for 2 minutes. Add to bowl with nuts.
6. Add paprika, salt, and pepper to bowl. Mix well. Store in an airtight glass container up to one month.

Tahini Maple Syrup GF | DF | EF | NF

This delicious syrup is rich with good fats, thanks to the tahini. It's great spooned over Sweet Potato Silver Dollars (see Chapter 7), oatmeal, toast, and much more.

YIELDS ½ CUP | Prep Time: 5 minutes | Cook Time: n/a

¼ cup tahini
¼ cup pure maple syrup

PER SERVING

(Serving size: 1 teaspoon)

Calories: 22 · Fat: 1g

Protein: 0g · Sodium: 2mg

Fiber: 0g · Carbohydrates: 3g

Net Carbs: 3g · Sugar: 2g

1. In a small bowl, whisk together tahini and maple syrup until combined. If tahini is very thick, warming it gently over the stovetop will help to loosen it, making it easier to combine with the maple syrup.

2. Store in an airtight container in the refrigerator up to two weeks.

Lemon-Tahini Dressing   GF | DF | EF | NF

This makes a wonderful everyday salad dressing. It's also a great dip for crudités and is delicious drizzled over roasted vegetables.

YIELDS 5 TABLESPOONS | Prep Time: 5 minutes | Cook Time: n/a

3 tablespoons tahini
1½ tablespoons lemon juice
¼ teaspoon salt
2 teaspoons honey
¼ cup hot water

1. Combine all the ingredients in a glass jar with a tight-fitting lid.
2. Shake vigorously until all ingredients come together and you have a smooth and uniform dressing.
3. Store in an airtight container in the refrigerator up to two weeks.

PER SERVING

(Serving size: 1 teaspoon)

Calories: 20 · Fat: 1g

Protein: 1g · Sodium: 40mg

Fiber: 0g · Carbohydrates: 2g

Net Carbs: 2g · Sugar: 1g

Green Oil GF | DF | EF | NF | CT

This herby olive oil can be used in so many ways—as a dressing for salads, to marinate fish or chicken, to garnish soups, or as a sandwich spread. These three herbs are just a suggestion. Mix and match any other herbs you want as you stick to the ratio of ½ cup olive oil to 1 cup herbs.

Phytonutrient focus: Parsley is especially high in vitamins A, C, and K. Traditionally, it is said to be especially good for kidney health. It has a wide range of antioxidant flavonoids, including a super high concentration of apigenin, which has well-researched anticancer, antidiabetic, and calming properties (chamomile is also very rich in apigenin).

YIELDS 1 CUP | Prep Time: 5 minutes | Cook Time: n/a

½ cup extra-virgin olive oil
½ cup packed roughly chopped
    parsley
¼ cup rosemary leaves
¼ cup roughly chopped chives
1 teaspoon salt
3 cloves garlic, peeled

In a food processor, combine all ingredients and blend together until smooth. Store in a covered glass jar in the refrigerator up to one week or freeze up to six months.

PER SERVING
(Serving size: 1 teaspoon)
Calories: 20 · Fat: 2g
Protein: 0g · Sodium: 48mg
Fiber: 0g · Carbohydrates: 0g
Net Carbs: 0g · Sugar: 0g

Nut Crumbs GF | DF | EF

This is a nut-based, gluten-free breading that can be used to make fish sticks and chicken tenders. It also works as a substitute for bread crumbs in many recipes. You can double or triple this recipe and store it in the freezer up to three months. You may use all almond flour or another nut flour in place of the ground walnuts.

YIELDS 1¼ CUPS | Prep Time: 10 minutes | Cook Time: n/a

½ cup walnut pieces
⅔ cup almond flour
¼ cup cornmeal
2 teaspoons smoked paprika
1 tablespoon nutritional yeast
¼ teaspoon salt

1. Place walnuts in a mini food processor and grind about 1 minute until they are finely ground.
2. In a medium bowl, combine ground walnuts with almond flour, cornmeal, paprika, yeast, and salt, mixing well. Use immediately or keep in a sealed container in the refrigerator.

PER SERVING

(Serving size: 2 tablespoons)

Calories: 98 · Fat: 8g

Protein: 3g · Sodium: 59mg

Fiber: 2g · Carbohydrates: 6g

Net Carbs: 4g · Sugar: 1g

Vegetable Stock GF | DF | EF | NF

Homemade vegetable stock makes all the difference in many recipes, especially soups, stews, and risotto, replacing water with a more flavorful and nutritious brew. It is healthier than canned stocks or bouillon cubes and has a lighter flavor. Make some whenever you have extra vegetables or vegetable scraps in the refrigerator and freeze in small (2–4 cups) containers so you can use as needed.

YIELDS 9 CUPS | Prep Time: 10 minutes | Cook Time: 45 minutes

2 tablespoons olive oil
3 medium carrots, cut to 2" pieces
3 medium stalks celery, cut to 2" pieces
2 small onions
10 cups cold water
½ cup dried shiitake mushrooms
1 (3") piece dried kombu
2 bay leaves
1 bunch parsley stems, cut in half
1 teaspoon salt
½ teaspoon ground black pepper

1. In a large pot over medium heat, warm oil and then sauté carrots, celery, and onions 5 minutes.

2. Add water and all remaining ingredients. Bring to a boil and then reduce to a simmer 40 minutes.

3. Strain and discard solids, reserving liquid. Alternately, if desiring a stock that is more viscous and has a deeper flavor, purée about ⅓ of cooked vegetables (taking care to remove bay leaves) in a food processor or blender and add them back into the broth.

PER SERVING

(Serving size: 1 cup)

Calories: 22 · Fat: 2g

Protein: 0g · Sodium: 261mg

Fiber: 0g · Carbohydrates: 1g

Net Carbs: 0g · Sugar: 0g

Flax Eggs GF | DF | EF | NF | CT

For those who have an egg allergy, this recipe can be used as a substitute for one egg in recipes in which eggs are not the main ingredient, such as in baked goods and batters.

YIELDS THE EQUIVALENT OF 1 EGG | Prep Time: 5 minutes | Cook Time: n/a

1 tablespoon finely ground raw flaxseed
2½ tablespoons water

In a small bowl, mix ingredients and let sit 5 minutes (until mixture becomes gelatinous) before using in a recipe.

PER SERVING

Calories: 37 · Fat: 3g

Protein: 1g · Sodium: 2mg

Fiber: 2g · Carbohydrates: 2g

Net Carbs: 0g · Sugar: 0g

Berry Ginger Jam GF | DF | EF | NF

This recipe can be served on toast, mixed with yogurt, used as a sweetener in smoothies, spooned on top of oatmeal, and more. You can use any mix of berries or other fruits that you have on hand. Ginger gives it a kick (feel free to reduce the amount based on your preference).

Phytonutrient focus: Ginger has strong antimicrobial and anti-inflammatory properties due to its unique blend of phytochemicals, including one named gingerol. Through various mechanisms, it helps boost the function of your immune system so you can more effectively fight against bacteria and viruses.

YIELDS 6 CUPS | Prep Time: 10 minutes | Cook Time: 30 minutes

8 cups berries, fresh or frozen
1 cup water
4 medium pitted dates
1 tablespoon grated fresh ginger
¼ cup lemon juice
¼ cup chia seeds

1. In a large pot over medium heat, combine berries, water, dates, ginger, and lemon juice. Mash berries lightly while mixing.
2. Bring to a simmer and cook about 30 minutes.
3. Add chia seeds and stir. Remove from heat and cool.
4. This jam may be stored in the refrigerator in an airtight jar up to three weeks.

PER SERVING

(Serving size: 2 tablespoons)

Calories: 15 · Fat: 0g

Protein: 0g · Sodium: 0mg

Fiber: 1g · Carbohydrates: 3g

Net Carbs: 2g · Sugar: 2g

······ BABY FOOD ·······

For babies, add a small spoonful of jam to oats or other grains.

Apple-Raspberry Sauce GF | DF | EF | NF

This beautiful pink applesauce can be used to top pancakes, spread on toast, layered into a parfait, or as a simple snack with granola sprinkled on top for crunch. It will keep in an airtight container up to two weeks.

YIELDS 2 CUPS | Prep Time: 15 minutes | Cook Time: 30 minutes

4 cups chopped medium red apples (skin on)
1 cup water
2 tablespoons pure maple syrup
1 tablespoon apple cider vinegar
½ teaspoon ground cinnamon
¼ teaspoon ground ginger
1 pint raspberries

1. In a large pot over medium-low heat, combine apples, water, maple syrup, vinegar, cinnamon, and ginger.
2. Bring to a simmer. Cook about 20 minutes or until apples are tender.
3. Add raspberries and simmer another 10 minutes.
4. Transfer to a food processor and purée until slightly chunky. Enjoy immediately or cool to room temperature before refrigerating.

PER SERVING

(Serving size: ¼ cup)

Calories: 61 · Fat: 0g

Protein: 1g · Sodium: 1mg

Fiber: 3g · Carbohydrates: 15g

Net Carbs: 12g · Sugar: 10g

· · · · · · BABY FOOD · · · · · · ·

This applesauce is a wonderful baby food, just as it is.

· ·

CHAPTER 7

Breakfast

American breakfast tends to be full of foods that provide "quick" energy. A bowl of sugary cereal, a bagel or muffin, a cup of coffee, and we're off to face our long day. These refined carbs, sugars, and caffeine cause a quick blood sugar spike. Usually, that feels pretty good—at first. But within a couple of hours, as blood sugar crashes, the buzz wears off and we feel tired, unfocused, hungry, and cranky. This "blood sugar roller coaster" is especially impactful on kids' energy, attention, and mood. And over the long term, this pattern, and its accompanying insulin surges, pave the way for chronic inflammation.

Here's the fix: three things that stabilize glucose peaks and valleys and deliver sustainable energy that lasts to lunchtime are *proteins, good fats, and fiber*. These help you feel fuller longer, and they reduce the impact of insulin on the body, which reduces inflammation.

In this chapter, you'll find a variety of foods with proteins, good fats, and fiber, including eggs, tofu, whole milk yogurt, nuts and seeds, vegetables, fruits, beans, and whole grains. Even when you're in a pinch for time, remember *proteins, fats, and fiber*. Try almond butter on whole-wheat toast, yogurt with fruit and a handful of nuts, or a simple hard-boiled egg.

Turmeric Scrambled Eggs   GF | DF | NF

A touch of turmeric brightens scrambled eggs, both visually and flavor-wise. You may never go back to plain old eggs. To really punch up the flavor and anti-inflammatory nutrients, try sprinkling a teaspoon of our Dukkah spice blend (see Chapter 6) over the eggs once cooked.

Phytonutrient focus: Turmeric is a bright orange rhizome that has been used for centuries in India. Recently, it has gained notoriety because of research on its potent anti-inflammatory and anticancer qualities. It is most effective as a whole root or powder. Turmeric is also made more bioavailable (i.e., more accessible to your body) when combined with good fats and a pinch of black pepper, as here in this recipe.

SERVES 1 | Prep Time: 5 minutes | Cook Time: 3 minutes

2 large eggs
¼ teaspoon ground turmeric
¼ teaspoon salt
⅛ teaspoon ground black pepper
1 tablespoon olive oil

· · · · · · · BABY FOOD · · · · · · ·

Eliminate salt and pepper in this dish. Mash eggs further once cooked or purée with breast-milk or formula. Alternately, cook eggs in larger-sized pieces babies and toddlers can hold in their hands.

1. In a small bowl, whisk together eggs, turmeric, salt, and pepper.

2. In a small nonstick pan over medium heat, heat oil. Add egg mixture. Using rubber spatula, move eggs gently back and forth as they cook.

3. Once fully cooked, about 2–3 minutes, remove from heat and transfer to plate to serve.

PER SERVING

Calories: 264 · Fat: 22g · Protein: 13g · Sodium: 723mg
Fiber: 0g · Carbohydrates: 1g · Net Carbs: 1g · Sugar: 0g

Tofu Scramble GF | DF | EF | NF

To diversify your healthy morning proteins, try this alternative to scrambled eggs! This scramble is also delicious in a burrito, with black beans, Pico de Gallo (see Chapter 11), and avocados.

SERVES 4 | Prep Time: 15 minutes | Cook Time: 15 minutes

2 tablespoons extra-virgin olive oil
¼ cup small diced onions
½ cup small diced red bell pepper
1 pound extra-firm tofu, drained and crumbled
1 teaspoon ground turmeric
½ teaspoon garlic powder
½ teaspoon onion powder
¼ teaspoon ground black pepper
¼ teaspoon salt

1. In a medium-sized sauté pan over medium heat, warm oil.
2. Add onions and bell peppers. Sauté about 5 minutes or until soft.
3. Add tofu, turmeric, garlic powder, onion powder, black pepper, and salt.
4. Sauté about 10 minutes until warm and lightly golden brown.

PER SERVING

Calories: 172 · Fat: 12g · Protein: 10g
Sodium: 176mg · Fiber: 2g
Carbohydrates: 6g · Net Carbs: 4g
Sugar: 2g

······· BABY FOOD ·······

To make this baby food, be certain vegetables are very finely diced and eliminate salt and pepper. If needed, mash tofu further once cooked or purée with breastmilk or formula.

Breakfast Tostadas GF | DF | NF

These tostadas make a hearty breakfast and can also be a lunch or dinner item, served alongside a green salad. If you don't have time to make Pico de Gallo or Pinto Bean Dip (both in Chapter 11), replace with a good-quality store-bought salsa and refried beans. And in case of egg allergies, leave out the eggs and add extra bean dip.

SERVES 4 | Prep Time: 10 minutes | Cook Time: 10 minutes

3 tablespoons extra-virgin olive oil, divided
8 (6") corn tortillas
8 large eggs
¼ teaspoon salt
1½ cups Pinto Bean Dip (see Chapter 11)
1 cup Pico de Gallo (see Chapter 11)
1 medium avocado, peeled, pitted, and sliced

PER SERVING

Calories: 457 · Fat: 23g
Protein: 15g · Sodium: 855mg
Fiber: 7g · Carbohydrates: 48g
Net Carbs: 41g · Sugar: 4g

······· BABY FOOD ·······

Serve this dish "deconstructed" for babies and toddlers. Make eggs scrambled instead of fried and serve with the bean dip (texture adjusted for age) and avocado. You could also spread some of the bean dip on pieces of tortilla for a nice finger food.

1. In a large frying pan, heat 1 tablespoon oil over medium heat. Add 4 tortillas and cook until crispy on one side, about 3 minutes. Then flip tortillas and cook until crispy on the other side, another 2–3 minutes. Add another tablespoon oil to pan, repeat with remaining 4 tortillas. Place 2 tortillas on each of four plates.

2. Add remaining 1 tablespoon oil to pan. Crack eggs carefully into pan in one layer, sprinkle with salt, and cook eggs to desired doneness. Remove to a plate.

3. To assemble, smear 3 tablespoons Pinto Bean Dip on each tortilla. Top each tortilla with one egg and spoon 2 tablespoons Pico de Gallo on top. Garnish with a few slices of avocado.

Savory Egg and Bulgur Muffins NF

These egg muffins are a great way to use leftover cooked vegetables and grains. Feel free to substitute other vegetables. To make it gluten-free, use cooked quinoa in place of bulgur. To make it dairy-free, use a milk alternative and remove the cheese. The muffins can be made ahead of time and stored in an airtight container in the refrigerator. Reheat in a toaster oven or microwave for a quick protein-rich breakfast. If you are using already cooked bulgur, you will need about ½ cup.

YIELDS 8 MUFFINS | Prep Time: 20 minutes | Cook Time: 1 hour 15 minutes

¼ cup bulgur
2 tablespoons olive oil
½ cup finely sliced shiitake mushrooms
½ cup finely chopped broccoli
4 large eggs
¼ cup whole milk
¼ cup shredded Cheddar cheese
½ teaspoon ground turmeric
¼ teaspoon salt
¼ teaspoon ground black pepper

····· BABY FOOD ·····

This recipe is appropriate for babies with adequate chewing skills. Alternately, sauté broccoli and mushrooms together and mash or purée with breast-milk or formula to desired consistency.

1. Preheat oven to 325°F. Grease an eight-cup muffin tin with cooking spray.

2. To cook bulgur, in a small saucepan, combine bulgur with ½ cup boiling water and let steep, covered, until tender, about 1 hour. Pour off any excess water. If in a rush, boil bulgur, uncovered, until tender, about 12 minutes.

3. In a small sauté pan over medium heat, heat oil. Add mushrooms and broccoli. Cook about 5 minutes until soft.

4. In a small bowl, whisk eggs and milk together. Add cooked bulgur, cheese, turmeric, salt, and pepper.

5. Distribute egg mixture evenly across eight muffin cups and then do the same with the vegetables. Place in oven and bake 8 minutes or until cooked through.

6. Remove from pan and serve hot or cool before storing.

PER SERVING
(Serving size: 1 muffin)

Calories: 104 · Fat: 7g · Protein: 5g · Sodium: 137mg · Fiber: 1g

Carbohydrates: 5g · Net Carbs: 4g · Sugar: 1g

Baked Cured Salmon GF | DF | EF | NF

Smoked salmon is a breakfast staple, but also a sodium bomb. Curing and cooking the salmon yourself makes a healthier breakfast option. It can be baked, grilled, or sautéed and served warm or chilled. It makes a great bagel topping, salmon salad base, or addition to a green salad at lunch or dinner.

SERVES 4 | Prep Time: 5 minutes, 24 hours passive | Cook Time: 20 minutes

1 (12-ounce) salmon fillet
1 tablespoon pure maple syrup
1 tablespoon coarse salt
½ cup roughly chopped dill

PER SERVING

Calories: 127 · Fat: 5g · Protein: 17g
Sodium: 622mg · Fiber: 0g
Carbohydrates: 2g · Net Carbs: 0g
Sugar: 2g

······· BABY FOOD ·······

Skip the curing step for babies and bake the salmon plain. This changes the texture, but it's still delicious. Small flakes of fish make good finger food. Or mash or purée together with a vegetable of your choice, such as sweet potato.

1. Rub salmon with maple syrup on all sides and sprinkle evenly with salt.
2. Press dill into salmon on both sides and put in an airtight container or plastic zipper bag. Keep refrigerated for 24 hours to cure.
3. Preheat oven to 375°F. Grease an 8" × 8" casserole dish.
4. Remove salmon from cure, rinse with cold water, and pat dry. Transfer to casserole dish.
5. Bake, uncovered, until salmon is flaky and cooked through, approximately 20 minutes.

Anti-Inflammatory Granola GF | DF | EF | CT

This is a versatile granola recipe that will become a family favorite. Unlike most store-bought granolas, it is low in sugar and has a lot of anti-inflammatory ingredients, including olive oil, dried cherries, and nuts and seeds (leave out the pecans to make it nut-free). Kids especially love it in a parfait with yogurt and fresh fruit, which they can make themselves. This recipe is not appropriate for babies.

YIELDS 4 CUPS | Prep Time: 15 minutes | Cook Time: 20 minutes

2 cups rolled oats (not instant)
1 cup chopped pecans
½ cup sunflower seeds
¼ cup sesame seeds
¼ teaspoon salt
1 teaspoon Sweet Spice Blend (see Chapter 6)
¼ teaspoon ground ginger
¼ cup extra-virgin olive oil
¼ cup pure maple syrup
¼ cup hemp hearts
½ cup dried cherries

PER SERVING

(Serving size: ¹/₂ cup)

Calories: 388 · Fat: 26g · Protein: 8g

Sodium: 75mg · Fiber: 5g

Carbohydrates: 34g · Net Carbs: 29g

Sugar: 14g

1. Preheat oven to 300°F. Line a baking sheet with parchment paper.
2. In a medium bowl, combine oats, pecans, sunflower seeds, sesame seeds, salt, Sweet Spice Blend, and ginger. Add oil and maple syrup and mix. Mixture may appear dry and crumbly but will crisp up in oven.
3. Pour mixture onto baking sheet and press granola into an even layer.
4. Bake 15–20 minutes or until dry and lightly browned.
5. Remove from oven and let cool 10 minutes. Then, using a metal spatula, remove from pan, taking care to keep some clusters intact. Combine with hemp hearts and cherries.

Chicken and Tofu Sausage

GF | DF | EF | NF

For this recipe, you will need extra-firm tofu. If packed in water, drain and press for at least 30 minutes to achieve the best texture. If you don't have sage on hand, don't let that stop you—this dish is still delicious without it.

YIELDS 8 PATTIES | Prep Time: 20 minutes | Cook Time: 15 minutes

1 (8-ounce) package extra-firm tofu, roughly chopped
8 ounces ground chicken
½ teaspoon salt
¼ teaspoon ground black pepper
¼ teaspoon ground turmeric
½ teaspoon ground sage
2 tablespoons olive oil

PER SERVING
(Serving size: 2 patties)

Calories: 185 · Fat: 13g

Protein: 14g · Sodium: 335mg

Fiber: 1g · Carbohydrates: 2g

Net Carbs: 1g · Sugar: 0g

· · · · · · · BABY FOOD · · · · · · ·

This dish is appropriate as a finger food for those with adequate chewing skills.

· ·

1. In the bowl of a food processor, add tofu. Pulse three to five times until tofu is ground to the texture of meat. Add to a large bowl.

2. To the bowl, add chicken, salt, pepper, turmeric, and sage. Mix until meat is fully incorporated with tofu.

3. Flatten mixture into an even layer. With hands, make marks to divide the mixture into eight portions. Roll each portion into a ball and flatten into a patty. Place on a plate until ready to cook.

4. In a large sauté pan over medium heat, warm oil. Working in batches if necessary, cook patties 6–8 minutes per side until golden brown and cooked through.

Overnight Oats with Chia

GF | DF | EF | NF | CT

For a combination of ease, health, and taste, it's hard to beat overnight oats! Oats and chia provide prebiotic fiber that encourages a healthy gut microbiome. Goji are super high in antioxidants (if you don't have them, use raisins instead). These oats are typically served cold, right out of the refrigerator. Make a big batch at night, and your family can help themselves to it for days to come. Add yogurt for protein and fat and top with fresh fruit.

YIELDS 5 CUPS | Prep Time: 10 minutes, passive overnight | Cook Time: n/a

2 cups rolled oats
¼ cup chia seeds
¼ cup goji berries
¼ cup chopped dates
¼ cup unsalted sunflower seeds
3 cups water

1. In a large glass container with a tight-fitting lid, combine all ingredients except water and mix well.
2. Add water, cover, and let sit in the refrigerator overnight.

PER SERVING

(Serving size: ½ cup)

Calories: 116 · Fat: 4g · Protein: 4g

Sodium: 7mg · Fiber: 4g

Carbohydrates: 17g · Net Carbs: 13g

Sugar: 4g

· · · · · · · BABY FOOD · · · · · · ·

Make a batch for your baby that combines just oats and chia seeds with milk of choice (including breastmilk). Eliminate the seeds and dried fruit, as those may be choking hazards.

· ·

Banana Quinoa Muffins CT

This is a substantial and nutritious muffin that you can feel good about serving for breakfast with yogurt or a smoothie. You can substantially reduce prep time by using leftover quinoa from another meal. If you wish, substitute gluten-free flour or Flax Eggs (see Chapter 6), or remove the nuts.

YIELDS 12 MUFFINS | Prep Time: 30 minutes | Cook Time: 50 minutes

½ cup raw quinoa (or 2 cups cooked quinoa)
1 cup water
2 medium bananas, peeled and mashed
2 large eggs
½ cup plain, whole milk yogurt
⅓ cup Sucanat (or sugar)
1 teaspoon vanilla extract
½ cup chopped walnuts
⅓ cup golden raisins
1 cup whole-wheat flour
2 teaspoons baking powder
½ teaspoon ground cinnamon
¼ teaspoon salt

PER SERVING

(Serving size: 1 muffin)	
Calories: 175 · Fat: 5g	
Protein: 5g · Sodium: 151mg	
Fiber: 3g · Carbohydrates: 29g	
Net Carbs: 26g · Sugar: 11g	

· · · · · · BABY FOOD · · · · · · ·

Make plain quinoa and mash it together with banana and a touch of cinnamon.

1. Rinse quinoa thoroughly. In a medium pot, combine quinoa and water. Bring to a boil, then cover and reduce heat to low. Simmer 18–20 minutes until all of the water has been absorbed and quinoa grains have opened. Turn off heat and let stand 5 minutes.

2. In the meantime, preheat oven to 350°F. Grease and flour a muffin pan or use muffin tin liners.

3. In a large bowl, combine mashed bananas, eggs, yogurt, Sucanat, and vanilla extract. Add cooked quinoa, walnuts, and raisins. Mix well.

4. In another large bowl, whisk together flour, baking powder, cinnamon, and salt.

5. Add flour mixture to banana mixture and stir just until combined. Do not overmix.

6. Fill each muffin mold with ⅓ cup batter.

7. Bake 25–30 minutes or until the tops are golden brown. Remove from oven and let muffins cool at least 15 minutes before serving. Reserve extras in an airtight container at room temperature up to two days or in the refrigerator up to five days.

Amaranth-Millet Porridge GF | DF | EF | NF

This porridge combines two whole grains that are exceptionally nutritious. Amaranth, like its cousin quinoa, is a "complete" protein. Millet is an ancient grain and still a staple in many African cuisines. Together, they have a range of flavonoids and other antioxidants with powerful anti-inflammatory qualities. Soaking the grains overnight improves their digestibility and shortens cooking time. Serve with Sweet Spiced Ghee (see Chapter 6) to add good fats and with other toppings, like yogurt, fruit, and nuts.

YIELDS 6 CUPS | Prep Time: 5 minutes | Cook Time: 30 minutes, passive overnight

1 cup amaranth
1 cup millet
7 cups water
¼ teaspoon salt

PER SERVING
(Serving size: ¹/₂ cup)

Calories: 112 · Fat: 2g

Protein: 4g · Sodium: 49mg

Fiber: 2g · Carbohydrates: 23g

Net Carbs: 21g · Sugar: 0g

· · · · · · · BABY FOOD · · · · · · ·

This porridge is a perfect baby food as is! You may want to loosen or thin it with milk of choice, including breastmilk.

· ·

1. Combine all ingredients in a large pot and let soak overnight.
2. In the morning, bring to a boil over medium-high heat.
3. Reduce heat to low and cook covered 30 minutes, stirring frequently to make sure mixture does not stick to the bottom of the pot.
4. Serve hot or cool down before storing in the refrigerator up to five days. In the morning, simply warm in a pan with toppings of your choice.

Buckwheat-Applesauce Pancakes GF | NF | CT

These nutty buckwheat pancakes are delicious with Tahini Maple Syrup (see Chapter 6). If you wish, you may use whole-wheat flour in place of the gluten-free blend. And to accommodate dairy or egg allergies, use a milk alternative and Flax Eggs (see Chapter 6).

YIELDS 12 PANCAKES | Prep Time: 15 minutes | Cook Time: 25 minutes

1 cup gluten-free flour blend, such as Bob's Red Mill
1 cup buckwheat flour
¼ teaspoon salt
1 tablespoon baking powder
1 teaspoon ground cinnamon
2 large eggs
2 cups whole milk
1 cup applesauce
1 medium apple, diced small
2 tablespoons pure maple syrup
2 tablespoons coconut oil, divided

1. In a medium bowl, combine the flours, salt, baking powder, and cinnamon.

2. In another medium bowl, whisk together eggs, milk, applesauce, apple pieces, and maple syrup. Add the dry ingredients to the wet and stir until just combined.

3. Heat a griddle or large sauté pan over medium heat. Melt 1 teaspoon oil. Using a small ladle, portion the pancakes onto pan or griddle (you should be able to cook at least two at a time). Cook until both sides are golden brown, about 1 minute per side. Repeat with remaining oil and batter.

PER SERVING

(Serving size: 2 pancakes)

Calories: 298 · Fat: 9g

Protein: 9g · Sodium: 402mg

Fiber: 5g · Carbohydrates: 47g

Net Carbs: 42g · Sugar: 16g

· · · · · · · BABY FOOD · · · · · · ·

These pancakes make a nice finger food for babies, minus the diced apple, which can be a choking hazard.

Sweet Potato Silver Dollars GF | EF | NF

Think of this dish as a nutrient-packed alternative to pancakes. It's *so* yummy! Make it easy by baking a batch of sweet potatoes on the weekend and using as needed throughout the week. They are easiest to slice when cold. Top with Tahini Maple Syrup (see Chapter 6) or yogurt. This is easily (and deliciously) made dairy-free by using coconut oil in place of butter.

Phytonutrient focus: Sweet potatoes have anticancer, antidiabetic, and anti-inflammatory qualities. They are especially high in B vitamins, iron, potassium, and beta-carotene (found in many orange vegetables). Perhaps the best thing about sweet potatoes is that they are deliciously sweet but also high in fiber, so those sugars are digested slowly in the body.

SERVES 4 | Prep Time: 25–45 minutes |
Cook Time: 10 minutes (once sweet potatoes are baked)

2 medium sweet potatoes
2 tablespoons butter, divided

PER SERVING
Calories: 106 · Fat: 5g

Protein: 1g · Sodium: 36mg

Fiber: 2g · Carbohydrates: 13g

Net Carbs: 11g · Sugar: 3g

· · · · · · · BABY FOOD · · · · · · ·

These silver dollars make a great finger food for babies.

1. The night before, bake sweet potatoes whole in a 400°F oven for 25–45 minutes until easily pierced with a fork.

2. Cool sweet potatoes to room temperature and then refrigerate them in an airtight container. Sweet potatoes can be stored up to four days.

3. Remove sweet potatoes from refrigerator. Using a sharp knife, slice into rounds approximately ½" thick. Try to keep the skin attached, as this helps them hold together.

4. In a medium frying pan over medium heat, warm 1 tablespoon butter. Add sweet potato slices in a single layer.

5. Cook on one side until browned and crispy, approximately 2–3 minutes, then flip each round and cook on the other side. Repeat with remaining butter and sweet potatoes.

CHAPTER 8

Lunch

Lunch can be a pain point for many families. Most of us are not at home at lunchtime, so it can be tempting to go with the path of least resistance, grabbing something quick in a convenience store, fast-food restaurant, or cafeteria. One secret to an easy lunch is leftovers. Many of the recipes in this chapter are designed to do double duty as delicious dinner entrees and pack easily for lunch the next day. Pair the Nut-Coated Chicken Tenders, Black Bean Burgers, or Tempeh Sticks with Cilantro Dip with a couple of sides, and you have a well-rounded dinner. The next day, the leftovers make a great sandwich or addition to a salad. Other recipes, like Green 'n' Beans Quesadillas or Mackerel Salad Sandwich are easy enough to put together in the morning, and soups can pack well in a thermos. Vegetable Pita Pizzas and Vegetable Summer Rolls also make fun cooking activity for kids on the weekend.

When you can't pack lunch, it's a good opportunity for both kids and adults to practice making healthy choices out of the house. Follow all the same anti-inflammatory guidelines—whole, plant-based foods first. Fortunately, America's lunch spots are getting hipper to healthier lunch options. Many school systems are also working to improve school lunch, and more advocacy from parents will continue to push this forward!

Baked Tofu Squares with Peanut Sauce   DF | EF | GF

This is irresistibly tasty tofu! It packs well in a lunchbox, accompanied by cut vegetable sticks and extra peanut sauce to dip them. This recipe makes more peanut sauce than you'll need for just the tofu, so you'll definitely have some left over for dipping. People who say they don't like tofu often haven't had it prepared in a tasty way. If you are skeptical, try this recipe.

SERVES 4 | Prep Time: 20 minutes | Cook Time: 30 minutes

1 pound extra-firm tofu
2 tablespoons toasted sesame oil
½ teaspoon salt
½ teaspoon ground black pepper
¼ teaspoon ground turmeric
¼ cup creamy unsweetened peanut butter
1 tablespoon apple cider vinegar
1 tablespoon gluten-free tamari
1 teaspoon honey
2 teaspoons grated fresh ginger
3 tablespoons water

······· BABY FOOD ·······

These tofu squares make great finger food for babies (cut into 2"–3" pieces), or you can mash the tofu once it is cooked. Honey is not recommended for babies under twelve months because of the risk of botulism, so make sure to eliminate it.

1. Preheat oven to 400°F.
2. Drain the liquid off tofu and pat it dry with paper towels. Cut into 1" cubes.
3. In a large bowl, combine oil, tofu, salt, pepper, and turmeric. Toss to coat tofu in seasonings. Transfer to a baking sheet, spreading into a single layer.
4. Bake tofu 20–30 minutes, turning occasionally until all sides are crisp.
5. In a medium bowl, combine peanut butter, vinegar, tamari, honey, ginger, and water. Whisk until smooth.
6. Serve tofu immediately with sauce.

PER SERVING

Calories: 269 · Fat: 20g · Protein: 15g · Sodium: 571mg
Fiber: 2g · Carbohydrates: 7g · Net Carbs: 5g · Sugar: 3g

Vegetable Summer Rolls   DF | EF | CT | NF | GF

On a hot summer day when no one feels like cooking, this is a satisfying vegan lunch. It lends itself well to custom blends of ingredients where kids can choose their favorite vegetables and is great for engaging kids in assembly. A great addition to these rolls is ½ cup kraut or another fermented vegetable.

SERVES 6 | Prep Time: 30 minutes | Cook Time: n/a

¼ cup gluten-free tamari
1 tablespoon white miso paste
1 tablespoon tahini
1 teaspoon rice vinegar
¼ teaspoon ground black pepper
¼ teaspoon ground turmeric
1 tablespoon water
24 (8") rice paper wrappers
1 medium red bell pepper, seeded
    and cut into thin strips
2 small carrots, cut into thin strips
1 small cucumber, cut into thin strips
½ recipe Baked Tofu Squares
    (see Baked Tofu Squares with
    Peanut Sauce recipe in this
    chapter), or 8 ounces plain
    firm tofu, cut into thin strips
1 cup frozen edamame, thawed

······· BABY FOOD ·······

This recipe is not appropriate for babies because raw vegetables can be choking hazards. Instead, offer your baby baked tofu and steamed or sautéed vegetables.

1. In a small bowl, whisk together tamari, miso, tahini, vinegar, black pepper, turmeric, and water to make dipping sauce. Set aside.

2. Fill a large bowl with warm water. Dip one rice paper wrapper in water and place on a clean cutting board or plate. Place a few strips of red peppers, carrots, cucumbers, tofu, and about 1 tablespoon edamame in the center of the wrapper. Fold sides in and roll tightly. Continue until all rolls are wrapped. While working, place each roll under a damp paper towel to keep rolls moist.

3. Serve immediately with dipping sauce or, to hold in refrigerator or lunchbox, place in an airtight container with a damp paper towel on top.

PER SERVING
(Serving size: 4 rolls)

Calories: 278 · Fat: 6g · Protein: 12g · Sodium: 1,062mg

Fiber: 4g · Carbohydrates: 44g · Net Carbs: 40g · Sugar: 3g

Nut-Coated Chicken Tenders GF | DF

These are quick, easy, and healthy chicken tenders. You can bake or pan-fry them—try both ways and let your family decide which they like best. Serve them in a sandwich with avocado, lettuce, and tomato or on top of a salad for a quick lunch or dinner. Swap eggs for Flax Eggs (see Chapter 6) if needed.

SERVES 4 | Prep Time: 8 minutes | Cook Time: 8–20 minutes

1 recipe (1¼ cups) Nut Crumbs
  (see Chapter 6)
1 large egg
¼ teaspoon salt
1 pound chicken tenders
2 tablespoons avocado oil (if pan-frying; 1 tablespoon if baking)

PER SERVING

(Pan-frying method)	
Calories: 332 · Fat: 27g	
Protein: 22g · Sodium: 349mg	
Fiber: 3g · Carbohydrates: 11g	
Net Carbs: 8g · Sugar: 1g	

······ **BABY FOOD** ······

Rather than serving babies these chicken fingers, remove a small portion of the raw chicken and boil it until well cooked with carrots and celery. Shred chicken, mash vegetables, and serve with a little olive oil or purée if needed.

1. Put Nut Crumbs in a medium shallow bowl.

2. In another medium shallow bowl, beat together egg with salt.

3. Working with one chicken strip at a time, dip in the egg batter, letting excess egg drip off, and then coat it with nut mixture, patting mixture into chicken firmly so it sticks.

4. At this point, bake or pan-fry them. If baking, place chicken tenders on a baking sheet. Drizzle 1 tablespoon oil over them and bake at 350°F for 15–20 minutes, depending on size of tenders. Chicken is done when it is white all the way through and there is no pink when it is cut into the thickest part.

5. If pan-frying, heat 2 tablespoons oil in a large pan over medium heat for 30 seconds. Keep heat low enough so oil does not smoke. Place tenders in pan in a single layer, not crowding them. Work in batches if necessary. Cook until the undersides are browned and crispy, about 4 minutes. Then turn over and cook about 4 minutes on the other side until fully cooked and white all the way through.

Mackerel Salad Sandwich DF | EF | NF

Think of this as a substitute for tuna salad. From the perspective of sustainability, nutrition, and taste, mackerel is a smart choice—it is an excellent source of omega-3 fats. A generous dose of lemon, capers, and avocado tames the fish taste, especially for kids who are still getting used to it. Substitute with gluten-free bread if needed.

SERVES 2 | Prep Time: 5 minutes | Cook Time: n/a

1 (4.25-ounce) can mackerel in olive oil, drained

2 tablespoons lemon juice

½ teaspoon capers

⅛ teaspoon salt

½ medium avocado, peeled, pitted, and mashed

4 slices tomato

4 lettuce leaves

4 slices whole-grain bread

1. In a small bowl, combine mackerel, lemon juice, capers, salt, and avocado. With a fork, break up mackerel into small pieces and mix well, coating it evenly with the other ingredients.
2. Assemble sandwiches with mackerel salad, tomato, and lettuce on bread.

PER SERVING

Calories: 295 · Fat: 9g

Protein: 19g · Sodium: 619mg

Fiber: 7g · Carbohydrates: 33g

Net Carbs: 27g · Sugar: 5g

· · · · · · BABY FOOD · · · · · · ·

This recipe is good for babies, minus the capers and salt. Mash the mackerel salad very well.

Vegetable Pita Pizzas EF | NF | CT

This is a perfect recipe to cook with kids, either as a simple lunch for one or at a party with a large group. Kids can safely cut the vegetables and cheese with plastic knives (with supervision) and layer the ingredients onto the pita themselves. Like so many of our recipes, this one is infinitely customizable. Other great vegetable choices are baby spinach and blanched broccoli.

SERVES 4 | Prep Time: 15 minutes | Cook Time: 10 minutes

4 whole-wheat pitas

½ pound mozzarella cheese, cut in ¼" cubes, or shredded

1 large tomato, sliced thin

¼ medium green bell pepper, sliced thin

4 shiitake mushrooms, stems removed and sliced thin

¼ medium onion, peeled and sliced thin

8 leaves fresh basil, finely cut

2 tablespoons extra-virgin olive oil

½ teaspoon dried oregano

¼ teaspoon salt

¼ teaspoon ground black pepper

1. Preheat oven to 400°F.
2. Evenly layer ingredients on each pita in the following order: half of cheese, tomato slices, other vegetables, remaining cheese, and finally top with basil.
3. Evenly distribute oil, oregano, salt, and pepper over top of pizzas.
4. Place pitas on a sheet tray lined with parchment paper. If making for a large group, write each person's name on the parchment next to their pita pizza.
5. Bake 10 minutes until edges of pitas are browned and cheese is melted.

PER SERVING

Calories: 392 · Fat: 16g · Protein: 21g · Sodium: 784mg

Fiber: 6g · Carbohydrates: 41g · Net Carbs: 35g · Sugar: 2g

· · · · · · BABY FOOD · · · · · · ·

This recipe is appropriate for children over two years or for younger babies with adequate chewing skills. For babies still on purées, cook shiitake mushrooms in a bit of olive oil and purée with breastmilk or formula.

White Bean Hummus and Quick Pickle Pita DF | EF | NF

Any bean can be puréed in this hummus style. The pickles are similarly versatile and a great way to use vegetable scraps from other dishes. Use gluten-free bread if needed.

SERVES 4 | Prep Time: 20 minutes | Cook Time: n/a

½ cup tahini

1 medium lemon, zested and juiced

1 teaspoon salt

½ teaspoon cumin

1 clove garlic, peeled

⅓ cup ice water

1 (15-ounce) can cannellini beans, drained and rinsed

4 whole-wheat pitas

2 cups Quick Vegetable Pickles, drained (see Chapter 10)

1. In the bowl of a food processor, combine tahini, lemon zest and juice, salt, cumin, and garlic. Turn machine on and gradually drizzle ice water into tahini mix.

2. Add beans and blend until very smooth, about 2 minutes.

3. Cut each pita in half. Warm in a toaster oven or quickly heat in a skillet.

4. Fill each pita half with ¼ cup hummus and ¼ cup Quick Vegetable Pickles. Serve immediately or pack in a lunchbox.

······ **BABY FOOD** ·······

White Bean Hummus is a wonderful baby food! Remember to use less salt if you are making this for a baby. Feed it to babies as a purée on its own, and/or use it as a nutritious add-on to any other purée. For finger feeders, use it as a dip or spread.

PER SERVING

Calories: 495 · Fat: 15g · Protein: 21g · Sodium: 1,096mg
Fiber: 15g · Carbohydrates: 72g · Net Carbs: 57g · Sugar: 4g

Green 'n' Beans Quesadillas   GF | EF | NF | CT

These are hearty and nutrient-packed quesadillas that kids (and adults) will love. Like the Vegetable Pita Pizzas, they are easy to customize and assemble so even young kids can shape their lunch and feel comfortable in the kitchen. Note that another way to cook them after they're assembled is to brush tortillas on both sides with olive oil and bake in the oven or toaster oven until they are lightly browned on top.

SERVES 4 | Prep Time: 8 minutes | Cook Time: 20 minutes

2 tablespoons extra-virgin olive oil, divided
1 clove garlic, peeled and finely chopped
1 cup finely chopped broccoli florets and tender stems
2 cups packed baby spinach leaves
½ teaspoon salt
1 (8-ounce) can black beans, rinsed and drained
½ pound shredded Cheddar cheese
8 (6"–8") corn tortillas
1 cup Pico de Gallo (see Chapter 11)

······· BABY FOOD ·······

As is, this recipe is appropriate for children over two years or for younger babies with adequate chewing skills. For others, steam the spinach and broccoli and mash or purée with some breastmilk or formula.

1. In a large frying pan over medium heat, heat 1 tablespoon oil and garlic for 30 seconds until garlic is just fragrant but not browned.

2. Add broccoli, spinach, salt, and about 2 tablespoons water. Cook 8 minutes until vegetables are soft and wilted. If they become dry during cooking, add a bit more water, 1 tablespoon at a time. Remove vegetables to a medium-sized bowl and wipe pan clean to use again for quesadillas.

3. Distribute the vegetables, beans, and cheese evenly across 4 tortillas. Cover them (like a sandwich) with other 4 tortillas.

4. Return pan to medium heat. Add remaining oil to pan. Place two quesadillas in pan. Cook 2–3 minutes or until the underside is lightly browned.

5. Carefully flip and cook on the other side an extra 2–3 minutes. Repeat with remaining quesadillas.

6. Cut quesadillas into quarters and serve hot, topped with Pico de Gallo.

PER SERVING

Calories: 459 · Fat: 25g · Protein: 21g · Sodium: 925mg

Fiber: 8g · Carbohydrates: 35g · Net Carbs: 27g · Sugar: 2g

Tempeh Sticks with Cilantro Dip GF | DF | EF | NF

Cooking tempeh this way takes just a few minutes and yields a crispy and lightly salty finger food—the same attributes that make chips so enticing!

Phytonutrient focus: The cilantro plant yields two distinct herbs: the green leaves (cilantro) and the seeds (coriander). The leaves are rich in vitamins A and K, and both are high in linalool, which helps maintain steady blood sugar and reduce cholesterol. Use coriander to lend flavor at the beginning of cooking, and sprinkle cilantro leaves in at the end of cooking.

SERVES 4 | Prep Time: 15 minutes | Cook Time: 6–8 minutes

1 large bunch cilantro
2 tablespoons tahini
2 teaspoons miso
1 tablespoon lemon juice
1 tablespoon pure maple syrup
1 teaspoon apple cider vinegar
¾ teaspoon salt, divided
2 tablespoons coconut oil
1 (8-ounce) package tempeh, cut crosswise into ¼" strips

········ BABY FOOD ·····

This cilantro dip is a great way to introduce bold new flavors to your baby (just use less salt). The tempeh is great for kids over two years or for younger babies with adequate chewing skills. For younger ones, serve with plain, uncooked tofu.

1. Trim and discard stem tips of cilantro. Break bunch in half with your hands, rinse well, and place in the bowl of a food processor.

2. Add tahini, miso, lemon juice, maple syrup, vinegar, and ¼ teaspoon salt to food processor and process until smooth, stopping to scrape down the bowl a couple of times. Taste and adjust seasoning if desired. Set aside.

3. Heat oil in a large skillet over medium heat. Add tempeh strips, sprinkle with ¼ teaspoon salt, and cook 3–4 minutes until they are golden brown on the underside. Flip them (two forks work well for this), season with remaining salt, and cook on other side another 3–4 minutes. Add a bit more oil to pan if needed.

4. Place tempeh on a serving dish and spoon sauce over it. Or serve separately as sticks and dip.

PER SERVING

Calories: 230 · Fat: 15g · Protein: 12g · Sodium: 566mg

Fiber: 1g · Carbohydrates: 12g · Net Carbs: 11g · Sugar: 4g

Swiss Chard and Feta Frittata GF | NF

This frittata makes a great breakfast, lunch, or dinner. You can serve it hot or at room temperature. Many Italians like to make a frittata panini (sandwich) for lunch—just tuck a slice between bread and enjoy! To make it dairy-free, simply eliminate the milk and cheese.

SERVES 4 | Prep Time: 10 minutes | Cook Time: 30 minutes

3 tablespoons extra-virgin olive oil, divided
1 small onion, peeled and diced small
1 bunch fresh Swiss chard, leaves and tender stems, finely chopped
8 large eggs
2 tablespoons whole milk
½ teaspoon salt
¼ teaspoon ground black pepper
½ cup (about 4 ounces) crumbled feta cheese
2 tablespoons finely chopped fresh parsley

PER SERVING

(Serving size: 2 pieces)

Calories: 209 · Fat: 17g

Protein: 8g · Sodium: 577mg

Fiber: 1g · Carbohydrates: 4g

Net Carbs: 3g · Sugar: 2g

1. Preheat oven to 350°F.
2. In a 9" cast iron (or other oven-safe) skillet over medium-high heat, warm 1 tablespoon oil. Add onions and sauté 5 minutes. Add Swiss chard and sauté an additional 7 minutes until both onions and chard are very soft.
3. While vegetables are sautéing, whisk eggs in a medium bowl. Stir in milk, salt, pepper, feta, and parsley.
4. Add cooked chard to egg mixture in bowl. Stir to combine.
5. Return pan to heat. Add remaining 2 tablespoons oil and heat for 30 seconds. Then add eggs and vegetable mixture, making sure they are evenly distributed in pan.
6. Cook over medium-low heat 5 minutes. Then place pan in oven and cook another 10 minutes or until a toothpick inserted into the center of frittata comes out clean.
7. Carefully remove pan from oven. Cut into eight equal pieces like a pizza. Serve hot or let cool before storing in the refrigerator.

Vegetable Fried Rice GF | DF | NF

The key to a good fried rice is to use leftover rice. Freshly cooked rice doesn't hold its texture. Make two times the amount of rice you need for dinner one night, and the next day, this recipe comes together quickly. Fresh or frozen vegetables work equally well.

SERVES 4 | Prep Time: 15 minutes | Cook Time: 15 minutes

2 tablespoons untoasted sesame oil
1 cup finely diced carrot
2 teaspoons grated fresh ginger
3 cloves garlic, peeled and chopped
3 medium scallions, thinly sliced, white and green parts separated
4 shiitake mushroom caps, diced
3 cups cooked leftover brown rice
1 cup corn kernels
1½ cups green peas
3 cups spinach
2 large eggs, beaten
2 tablespoons gluten-free tamari
2 teaspoons toasted sesame oil
1 tablespoon brown rice vinegar
¼ teaspoon ground black pepper
½ cup roughly chopped kimchee

1. In a large wok or sauté pan, heat untoasted sesame oil over medium heat. Add carrots, ginger, garlic, whites from scallions, and mushrooms. Sauté 3–5 minutes until scallions are translucent.

2. Add cooked rice, breaking up the lumps. Add corn, peas, green parts of scallions, and spinach and sauté until spinach is wilted, about 3–5 minutes.

3. Make a well in the center of the rice, add eggs, and stir into rice until egg is cooked through, about 2–3 minutes. Remove from heat.

4. In a small bowl, whisk together tamari, toasted sesame oil, rice vinegar, and black pepper.

5. Add sauce and chopped kimchee to rice. Toss to combine and serve.

PER SERVING

Calories: 412 · Fat: 13g · Protein: 13g · Sodium: 830mg
Fiber: 9g · Carbohydrates: 62g · Net Carbs: 53g · Sugar: 10g

· · · · · · · BABY FOOD · · · · · · ·

This recipe contains fibrous vegetables (peas and corn) with a texture that is difficult for babies still learning to chew. But it will purée well with breastmilk or formula. Remove kimchee.

Black Bean Burgers DF | EF | NF

These plant-based burgers make a fun lunch and taste great at room temperature. To save time and energy, double the recipe, which will give you both a quick weeknight meal and leftovers. Serve on buns with lettuce, tomato, and other toppings of choice. To make them gluten-free, substitute bread crumbs with fine cornmeal or almond flour.

SERVES 4 | Prep Time: 20 minutes | Cook Time: 15–20 minutes

3 tablespoons avocado oil, divided
1 small carrot, cut finely into ⅛" dice
1 small stalk celery, cut finely into ⅛" dice
½ cup finely diced shiitake mushrooms
1 tablespoon gluten-free tamari
½ teaspoon cumin
½ teaspoon paprika
1 clove garlic, peeled and minced
1 (15-ounce) can black beans, drained and rinsed
¼ teaspoon salt
2 tablespoons unseasoned bread crumbs

1. Warm 1 tablespoon oil in a cast iron (or nonstick) skillet over medium heat and add carrot and celery. Cook 5 minutes.
2. Add mushrooms, tamari, cumin, paprika, and garlic. Cook another 5 minutes. Set aside.
3. Place beans in a medium bowl and mash well with a potato masher or fork. They should still have a coarse texture but come together in a sticky ball.
4. Add cooked vegetables, salt, and bread crumbs to the beans. Mix well.
5. Divide mixture into four equal portions and shape into burgers.
6. At this point, they can be cooked one of two ways: Brush them well with remaining 2 tablespoons oil and bake them in a 425°F oven 8–10 minutes. Or, to make them on the stovetop, heat remaining 2 tablespoons oil over medium heat in large cast iron pan. Add burgers and cook 4–5 minutes on each side. Take care when flipping—they are more likely than meat burgers to crumble apart.

······· BABY FOOD ·······

The burgers are good for babies twelve months and up or for those who can eat small pieces of soft solids. Make sure the vegetables are very finely cut so they are not choking hazards. The burger mashes up easily once cooked.

PER SERVING

Calories: 218 · Fat: 11g · Protein: 8g · Sodium: 672mg	
Fiber: 9g · Carbohydrates: 23g · Net Carbs: 14g · Sugar: 2g	

Pesto Pasta EF | CT

This pasta is delicious hot or at room temperature. Make it for dinner one night and send leftovers for lunch the next day. Experiment by swapping in your family's favorite vegetables—string beans (cut in 1" pieces), eggplant, and fresh corn in the summer are all great choices.

Phytonutrient focus: Basil is a highly aromatic herb with a long list of phenolic compounds. It has rosmarinic acid, caffeic acid, apigenin, and even cinnamyl. Together these phenols exert a strong antioxidant effect, protecting cells against oxidative damage. And they combine to form this wonderful fragrance and taste that is uniquely basil.

SERVES 6 | Prep Time: 15 minutes | Cook Time: 15 minutes

1 pound whole-wheat fusilli
2 tablespoons extra-virgin olive oil
2 cloves garlic, peeled and minced
1 small zucchini, diced medium
1 medium head broccoli, cut into small (1") florets
1 pint cherry tomatoes, cut in half
¾ teaspoon salt
⅛ teaspoon ground black pepper
1 cup Walnut Pesto (see Chapter 6)

······· BABY FOOD ·······

Purée or mash just the cooked vegetables with a bit of pesto and serve alone. For babies who can safely eat cooked noodles, serve the vegetable purée with pasta.

1. Bring a large pot of well-salted water to boil. Add pasta and cook until al dente or according to package instructions. Strain pasta, reserving 1 cup pasta water.

2. While pasta is cooking, heat oil in a large sauté pan over medium heat. Add garlic and sauté 30 seconds until it is fragrant but not browned. Add zucchini, broccoli, tomatoes, salt, and pepper. Cook 10–15 minutes until vegetables are tender. Check seasoning and remove from heat.

3. In a large bowl, combine pasta, vegetables, Walnut Pesto, and ¼ cup pasta water and gently mix until pasta is evenly coated with Walnut Pesto and vegetables. If it seems dry, add a bit more pasta water.

4. Serve hot or at room temperature.

PER SERVING

Calories: 407 · Fat: 27g · Protein: 10g · Sodium: 765mg
Fiber: 6g · Carbohydrates: 32g · Net Carbs: 26g · Sugar: 2g

Creamy Carrot Soup GF | DF | EF | NF

This soup gets its creamy texture not from dairy, but from coconut milk and blended cannellini beans, which also add protein and lots of phytonutrients. You may use this same formula for vegetables other than carrots, such as winter squash or sweet potatoes.

SERVES 8 | Prep Time: 10 minutes | Cook Time: 35 minutes

1 tablespoon minced fresh ginger
½ teaspoon Sweet Spice Blend (see Chapter 6)
1 pound carrots, roughly chopped
4 cups Vegetable Stock (see Chapter 6)
½ teaspoon salt
¾ cup canned cannellini beans, drained and rinsed
1 (14-ounce) can unsweetened coconut milk
1 tablespoon pure maple syrup
½ teaspoon ground black pepper

1. In a medium saucepan, combine ginger, Sweet Spice Blend, carrots, Vegetable Stock, and salt and bring to a boil. Reduce heat to medium and cook until carrots are soft enough so that a fork goes smoothly through, about 25–30 minutes.
2. Add cannellini beans, coconut milk, and maple syrup. Bring back to a boil for 2 more minutes.
3. Remove from heat, cool slightly, and transfer to a blender. Working in batches, blend until smooth or use an immersion blender. Season with pepper and serve hot.

PER SERVING

Calories: 166 · Fat: 11g
Protein: 3g · Sodium: 374mg
Fiber: 3g · Carbohydrates: 14g
Net Carbs: 11g · Sugar: 5g

· · · · · · · BABY FOOD · · · · · · ·

This soup makes a great baby food. Just use less salt and pepper.

· ·

Quinoa and Sweet Potato Bowls with Avocado Dressing GF | DF | EF | NF

This is a great meal to eat fresh or pack for lunch. If making ahead for lunch bowls, allow the sweet potatoes and quinoa to cool before packaging and refrigerating. The dressing is best if made no more than a day in advance. Note that the sweet potatoes roasted in this way also make a great dinner side dish.

SERVES 5 | Prep Time: 20 minutes | Cook Time: 30 minutes

2 large sweet potatoes, skin on, diced medium
2 tablespoons extra-virgin olive oil
¾ teaspoon salt, divided
1 tablespoon Tex-Mex Spice Blend, divided (see Chapter 6)
2 cups water
¾ cup quinoa
1 cup quartered cherry tomatoes
1¼ cups sauerkraut
½ cup thinly sliced red onion
1 recipe Avocado Dressing (see Chapter 6)

········ **BABY FOOD** ·······

Separate out some of the cooked quinoa and sweet potato for babies. Mash or blend together into a purée. Serve with avocado and a little lime and cumin.

1. Preheat oven to 350°F.
2. On a baking sheet, toss sweet potatoes with 2 tablespoons oil, ½ teaspoon salt, and 2 teaspoons Tex-Mex Spice Blend. Cook 30 minutes until outsides are browned and insides are soft.
3. Meanwhile, in a small pot, bring water and ¼ teaspoon salt to a boil. Stir in remaining teaspoon Tex-Mex Spice Blend. Add quinoa, cover with a lid, and simmer 12–15 minutes or until quinoa has absorbed all the liquid and is cooked through.
4. In five bowls or plastic lunch containers, evenly divide quinoa and sweet potatoes. Garnish with tomatoes, sauerkraut, and onion. Dress with Avocado Dressing immediately or place dressing in small, sealed containers to dress before serving.

PER SERVING

Calories: 303 · Fat: 16g · Protein: 6g · Sodium: 734mg

Fiber: 7g · Carbohydrates: 35g · Net Carbs: 28g · Sugar: 4g

Tomato Soup GF | EF | NF

Many kids love tomato soup, and it is full of wonderful antioxidants, like lycopene, that are found in tomatoes. If you want to make it dairy-free, simply leave out the crème fraiche. Garnish this soup with chopped herbs like chives or basil.

Phytonutrient focus: Tomatoes are a great source of vitamin C, folate, and potassium. They're also rich in a phytonutrient called lycopene, which has well-researched anticancer and heart-protective qualities. Lycopene is more bioavailable when tomatoes are cooked, and has greater protective effects against cardiovascular diseases when combined with olive oil. When tomatoes are raw, vitamin C is greater, so eat tomatoes all ways!

YIELDS 6 CUPS | Prep Time: 15 minutes | Cook Time: 40 minutes

2 tablespoons extra-virgin olive oil
2 medium leeks, white and light green parts only, cut into ½" half-moons (well rinsed)
3 medium carrots, cut in ½" pieces
3 medium celery stalks, cut in ½" pieces
1 (28-ounce) can puréed tomatoes
2 bay leaves
1 teaspoon salt
½ teaspoon ground black pepper
3 cups Vegetable Stock (see Chapter 6)
½ cup packed roughly chopped fresh basil leaves
¼ cup and 2 teaspoons crème fraiche

1. In a large pot over medium heat, combine oil and leeks and cook 5 minutes, stirring frequently until leeks are softened.
2. Add carrots and celery and continue sautéing another 3 minutes.
3. Add puréed tomatoes, bay leaves, salt, pepper, and Vegetable Stock. Bring to a boil. Then reduce heat to medium-low. Cook 25–30 minutes, stirring occasionally.
4. Add basil and turn off heat. Remove bay leaves and discard.
5. Working in batches, purée soup in a food processor or blender until it is very smooth.
6. Serve topped with a dollop of crème fraiche.

PER SERVING

(Serving size: 1 cup)

Calories: 178 · Fat: 10g · Protein: 4g · Sodium: 831mg

Fiber: 4g · Carbohydrates: 21g · Net Carbs: 17g · Sugar: 10g

Kimchee Grilled Cheese EF | NF | CT

Jazz up a simple grilled cheese with kimchee. You *and* your microbiome will be happy. If you want a less spicy ferment, try sauerkraut or other fermented vegetables. Use gluten-free bread if you wish.

SERVES 1 | Prep Time: 5 minutes | Cook Time: 5 minutes

2 slices whole-grain bread
1 tablespoon butter
2 (1-ounce) slices Cheddar cheese
2 tablespoons kimchee

PER SERVING

Calories: 512 · Fat: 29g

Protein: 22g · Sodium: 897mg

Fiber: 5g · Carbohydrates: 33g

Net Carbs: 28g · Sugar: 5g

1. Butter both sides of bread.
2. Make a sandwich with cheese and kimchee between bread, buttered sides facing out.
3. In a small skillet over medium-low heat, toast until golden on both sides and cheese is melted, about 2 minutes per side.

······· BABY FOOD ·······

For babies with adequate chewing skills, this can make good finger food, minus the kimchee.

CHAPTER 9

Dinner

For many families, dinner is the only meal they get to spend together. But getting a varied, satisfying meal on the table after a long day can be challenging. You will find that many of the dinners in this chapter are simple, requiring minimal chopping and tending. Most are forgiving in terms of cooking time and not too exacting regarding ingredients. If you look at the list of ingredients and don't have them all, remember the simple answer to making substitutions: "Sure!"

Most of these recipes are complete meals, best supplemented with nothing more complicated than a salad or cooked grains like rice or noodles. You will also find a couple of recipes that are more involved like the Butternut–Black Bean Enchilada Squares, which are great for weekends or special occasions. While nothing in this chapter needs a fancy kitchen tool, having a rice cooker (which reliably makes all kinds of grains), an Instant Pot®, or a pressure cooker to speed things along can be invaluable when everyone is "hangry" after work and school.

And remember, the context of your meals is just as important as what you eat. A relaxed and social dinnertime promotes well-being on all levels!

Eggplant Shakshuka GF | DF | NF

Shakshuka is a dish found throughout North Africa and the Mediterranean where eggs are poached in a spicy and rich tomato sauce. It is a great brunch entrée or easy vegetarian dinner. This version includes additional vegetables and spices. If you don't have canned tomatoes, you can always use 2 cups fresh diced tomatoes.

SERVES 4 | Prep Time: 15 minutes | Cook Time: 45 minutes

2 tablespoons olive oil

¾ cup onion (about ½ medium onion)

2 cloves garlic, peeled and minced

1 (15-ounce) can diced tomatoes

1½ cups medium diced red bell pepper

3 cups medium diced eggplant

1 tablespoon plus 1 teaspoon Basic Anti-Inflammatory Spice Blend (see Chapter 6)

⅓ cup tomato paste

1½ cups water

1¼ teaspoons salt

½ cup roughly chopped fresh basil, divided

6 large eggs

1. In a large (12") skillet, heat oil over medium heat.
2. Add onions and cook 3 minutes. Then add garlic and sauté another 30 seconds.
3. Add tomatoes, red pepper, eggplant, and Basic Anti-Inflammatory Spice Blend. Continue to cook over medium heat until vegetables sizzle. Cover and reduce to low heat. Cook 15 minutes.
4. Add tomato paste, water, and salt and return to a simmer. Cook another 15 minutes, covered.
5. Stir in ⅓ cup basil.
6. Carefully crack eggs on top of sauce and cover pot. Cook over low heat until eggs are cooked on the outside but still have a soft yellow center, about 8–10 minutes.
7. Serve with remaining basil as garnish.

······· BABY FOOD ·······

This recipe makes great baby food if you leave out or reduce the salt. Mash or purée further after cooking as needed.

PER SERVING

Calories: 265 · Fat: 14g · Protein: 13g · Sodium: 1,205mg			
Fiber: 7g · Carbohydrates: 22g · Net Carbs: 15g · Sugar: 11g			

Vegetable and Bean Chili   GF | EF | NF | CT

This is a hearty and satisfying one-pot meal that kids will love—and it makes excellent leftovers. The crumbled tempeh at the base lends a texture similar to ground meat. If you wish, you can make it dairy-free by eliminating the cheese.

SERVES 8 | Prep Time: 15 minutes | Cook Time: 35 minutes

2 tablespoons extra-virgin olive oil

1 (8-ounce) package tempeh, crumbled or cut into small pieces

1 small onion, peeled and diced small

2 cloves garlic, peeled and minced

2 tablespoons Tex-Mex Spice Blend (see Chapter 6)

1 teaspoon salt

1 cup small diced red bell pepper

1 cup small diced carrot

1 (15-ounce) can black beans, drained and rinsed

1 (15-ounce) can chickpeas, drained and rinsed

1 (15-ounce) can diced tomatoes

2 cups water

2 cups fresh or frozen corn kernels

⅓ cup chopped fresh cilantro

1 tablespoon lime juice

½ cup shredded Cheddar cheese

1. In a large pot over medium heat, heat oil and then sauté tempeh in it for 5 minutes until it browns.

2. Add onion, garlic, Tex-Mex Spice Blend, and salt and cook another 3 minutes, stirring frequently.

3. Add peppers, carrots, beans, chickpeas, tomatoes, and water. Cook 25 minutes.

4. Add corn and cook another 2 minutes. Then turn off heat.

5. Serve hot topped with cilantro, lime juice, and cheese.

PER SERVING

Calories: 270 · Fat: 9g · Protein: 15g · Sodium: 639mg
Fiber: 9g · Carbohydrates: 33g · Net Carbs: 24g · Sugar: 7g

· · · · · · BABY FOOD · · · · · · ·

This recipe makes great baby food if you leave out or reduce the salt. Mash or purée further after cooking as needed.

· ·

Dal with Cabbage and Carrots GF | DF | EF | NF |

This Indian-inspired recipe uses aromatic spices to enliven otherwise simple beans and vegetables. We recommend serving it with basmati rice and Indian-Spiced Spinach and Tofu (see recipe in this chapter). If you don't have nigella seeds, leave them out or add a bit more cumin seeds.

SERVES 4 | Prep Time: 15 minutes | Cook Time: 45 minutes

1 cup red split lentils

3 cups water

½ teaspoon turmeric

¾ teaspoon salt, divided

1 tablespoon coconut oil

½ teaspoon nigella seeds

½ teaspoon whole mustard seeds

½ teaspoon whole cumin seeds

½ teaspoon cumin powder

½ cup small diced onion

1 (1") piece fresh ginger, peeled and minced

2 cloves garlic, peeled and minced

2 cups shredded green cabbage

1 cup shredded carrot

½ cup diced tomato (canned or fresh)

1 tablespoon lemon juice

½ teaspoon Sweet Spice Blend (see Chapter 6)

½ cup chopped fresh cilantro

1. In a medium pot, combine lentils, water, turmeric, and ¼ teaspoon salt. Bring to a boil, then reduce to a simmer, and cook uncovered 20 minutes. Remove from heat.

2. In the meantime, in a large sauté pan over low heat, melt oil. Add nigella seeds, mustard seeds, cumin seeds, and cumin powder and gently toast for 30 seconds. Add onion and ginger and sauté 3 minutes. Add garlic and sauté another 30 seconds.

3. Add cabbage, carrots, tomato, and remaining ½ teaspoon salt. Stir until vegetables are well covered in the spices and begin to wilt down. Cover with a lid and cook 15–20 minutes. Vegetables are all cooked when cabbage is soft.

4. Add lentils plus whatever cooking water remains in pot to cabbage mixture. Add lemon juice, Sweet Spice Blend, and cilantro.

5. Cook 3 more minutes until the excess water is gone and the mixture is thick. Serve hot!

PER SERVING

Calories: 247 · Fat: 5g · Protein: 13g · Sodium: 522mg

Fiber: 8g · Carbohydrates: 41g · Net Carbs: 33g · Sugar: 4g

Fish Tacos GF | DF | EF | NF

Fish tacos are a great way to introduce fish to kids. Fish is usually fried for tacos, but here we bake it with anti-inflammatory herbs and spices. It's great served alongside a helping of brown rice and our Pinto Bean Dip (unblended) (see Chapter 11). Other nice additions are Guacamole and Pico de Gallo (see Chapter 11). Feel free to use any white fish in this recipe.

SERVES 4 | Prep Time: 20 minutes | Cook Time: 20–30 minutes

1 pound flounder fillets
¼ teaspoon salt
1 tablespoon Tex-Mex Spice Blend
(see Chapter 6)
2 tablespoons extra-virgin olive oil
2 tablespoons fresh lime juice
½ cup chopped scallions
½ cup chopped cilantro
8 (6") corn tortillas
½ recipe Fennel Slaw (see Chapter 10)

PER SERVING

Calories: 364 · Fat: 18g	
Protein: 20g · Sodium: 817mg	
Fiber: 5g · Carbohydrates: 31g	
Net Carbs: 26g · Sugar: 5g	

· · · · · · **BABY FOOD** · · · · · · ·

Serve the fish on its own. Eliminate the Fennel Slaw or cook the vegetables until they are soft and can be cut small or puréed.

· ·

1. Preheat oven to 350°F.
2. In a casserole dish, season fish with salt and Tex-Mex Spice Blend. Then add oil, lime juice, scallions, and cilantro, making sure fish is evenly coated on both sides.
3. Bake 15–20 minutes (depending on thickness of fillet) until fish is opaque white throughout and flakes easily with a fork. Using a large spoon, break up fish fillets into large chunks.
4. While fish is cooking, warm tortillas either in a skillet on the stovetop (30 seconds–1 minute each side), or you can stack them, wrap the stack in tin foil, and place them in oven about 7–8 minutes until warmed through.
5. Serve a portion of fish on each corn tortilla, top with slaw (and anything else you wish), and enjoy!

Indian-Spiced Spinach and Tofu GF | DF | EF | NF

This vegan version of the beloved saag paneer is a great way to get picky eaters interested in green vegetables—and comes together quickly for a weeknight dinner. For a more traditional version, use ghee and paneer cheese. Serve alongside Dal with Cabbage and Carrots (see recipe in this chapter) and basmati rice.

SERVES 4 | Prep Time: 10 minutes | Cook Time: 20 minutes

2 tablespoons coconut oil, divided
1¼ cups small diced onion
1 medium serrano pepper, diced small (use less if you want it less spicy)
3 cloves garlic, peeled and minced
1 (1") piece fresh ginger, peeled and minced
1¼ teaspoons salt, divided
½ teaspoon ground black pepper
1 teaspoon coriander
1 teaspoon turmeric
1 teaspoon Sweet Spice Blend (see Chapter 6)
¾ cup diced tomatoes (canned or fresh)
1 (10-ounce) package prewashed spinach
1 tablespoon fresh lemon juice
½ cup canned unsweetened coconut milk
½ pound extra-firm tofu, drained and cut into 1" cubes

1. Heat a large sauté pan over medium heat. Add 1 tablespoon oil, onion, and serrano pepper. Cook until onions are translucent, stirring frequently, about 5 minutes. Reduce heat to medium-low.

2. Add garlic, ginger, 1 teaspoon salt, black pepper, coriander, turmeric, and Sweet Spice Blend and cook about 1 minute or until aromatic. Add tomatoes and cook another 1 minute, stirring frequently.

3. Add spinach and cook until thoroughly wilted, about 3 minutes.

4. Place this mixture in a blender with lemon juice and milk. Pulse a few times until smooth.

5. Wipe out sauté pan. Add remaining 1 tablespoon oil and heat over medium-low heat for 1 minute. Add tofu cubes and season with ¼ teaspoon salt. Cook about 7 minutes, turning tofu so cubes are evenly golden brown. Add spinach back to pan with tofu and cook until warmed through.

PER SERVING
Calories: 220 · Fat: 15g · Protein: 9g · Sodium: 885mg
Fiber: 4g · Carbohydrates: 14g · Net Carbs: 10g · Sugar: 4g

Sicilian Pasta with Broccoli DF | EF

This recipe is inspired by Sicilian cooking, which often combines raisins, almonds, and tomato to make a sweet and savory sauce. It also has anchovies! This might make some of you want to turn the page, but trust us and try it! The way we do it hides any fishy taste, and you just get a base of umami flavor that makes us call anchovies "bacon of the sea" (albeit a much healthier version). Use gluten-free pasta and eliminate the almonds if needed.

SERVES 5 | Prep Time: 10 minutes | Cook Time: 15 minutes

2 pounds broccoli, cut into ½"
 pieces
1 pound whole-wheat fusilli
1 (2-ounce) tin anchovy fillets in
 olive oil
2 tablespoons extra-virgin olive oil
5 cloves garlic, peeled and minced
¼ cup plus 2 tablespoons tomato
 paste
¼ cup raisins
¼ cup roughly chopped almonds
¼ cup chopped fresh parsley

PER SERVING

Calories: 316 · Fat: 9g	
Protein: 14g · Sodium: 605mg	
Fiber: 10g · Carbohydrates: 50g	
Net Carbs: 40g · Sugar: 10g	

· · · · · · · BABY FOOD · · · · · · ·

This recipe is suitable for babies with appropriate chewing skills, minus the almonds.

1. Bring a large pot of salted water to a rolling boil. Add broccoli and cook 2–3 minutes. With a slotted spoon, remove broccoli from water, keeping water in pot.

2. Bring water back up to boil. Add pasta and cook according to instructions. When done, drain, reserving 2 cups cooking water.

3. While pasta is cooking, remove anchovies from oil and chop them finely. Then use the side of a knife to mash them into a paste. This is an easy process since they are very soft.

4. In a large sauté pan over low heat, add oil, anchovy paste, and garlic. Heat for 30 seconds-1 minute (do not allow garlic to brown), and then add tomato paste. Stir with a wooden spoon for 2 minutes.

5. Add broccoli and raisins and 1 cup pasta cooking water to pan. Cook 10 minutes or until broccoli is soft and well mixed with tomato.

6. Reduce heat to low. Add cooked pasta, almonds, and another ½ cup cooking water. Stir together gently 2 minutes.

7. Serve hot, garnished with parsley.

Salmon Poke Bowl GF | DF | EF | NF | CT

Poke bowls are traditionally made with raw fish, but here we cook the salmon in a tasty miso marinade. If you don't have fresh mango, feel free to use frozen mango cubes.

SERVES 4 | Prep Time: 15 minutes | Cook Time: 50 minutes

1¼ cups short-grain sticky brown rice, rinsed

2½ cups water

2 tablespoons miso

2 tablespoons gluten-free tamari

1 tablespoon toasted sesame oil

2 tablespoons extra-virgin olive oil

1 tablespoon plus 1 teaspoon honey

1 tablespoon minced ginger

2 teaspoons brown rice vinegar

½ teaspoon red pepper flakes

1 (1-pound) salmon fillet

1 cup medium diced mango

1 medium avocado, peeled, pitted, diced medium

1 cup drained Sweet Pickled Shiitake and Ginger (see Chapter 10)

¼ cup liquid from Sweet Pickled Shiitake and Ginger

¼ cup thinly sliced scallions

····· **BABY FOOD** ·····

Serve this recipe "deconstructed" for babies, with a small portion of rice, fish, mango, and avocado, cut to appropriate sizes or mashed. For babies under twelve months, eliminate the honey in the salmon marinade.

1. Preheat oven to 350°F. Line a medium-sized casserole dish or baking pan with parchment paper.

2. In a small pot, combine rice and water. Bring to a boil and then reduce to a simmer. Simmer with the lid on 30 minutes, undisturbed. When done, take off heat and let sit with lid on.

3. While rice cooks, in a small bowl, combine miso, tamari, sesame oil, olive oil, honey, ginger, vinegar, and pepper flakes. Mix well until combined.

4. Place salmon in dish or pan and pour the sauce over salmon. Coat it well on both sides and then place salmon skin-side down in baking dish.

5. Bake 15–20 minutes (depending on thickness) or until salmon flakes easily with a fork at the thickest part. Remove from oven and slice into 1"-thick strips.

6. Portion rice into four bowls (about 1 cup each). Arrange portions of salmon, mango, avocado, and Sweet Pickled Shiitake and Ginger each in their own sections around bowl. (This is a good step for kids to help with!)

7. Distribute the pickling liquid over the bowls, sprinkle with scallions and serve.

PER SERVING

Calories: 629 · Fat: 23g · Protein: 31g · Sodium: 1,414mg			
Fiber: 8g · Carbohydrates: 72g · Net Carbs: 64g · Sugar: 16g			

Pasta with Ricotta, Peas, and Mint EF | NF

This is a very quick weeknight dish. Using ricotta as a pasta sauce is a tried-and-true Italian technique to making a creamy pasta, and it also gives you more protein and less fat than heavy cream. The shells are a fun shape for kids, especially because the peas can snuggle inside them. Alternatives to peas include sautéed zucchini or Swiss chard, and you can use gluten-free pasta if you wish. Serve alongside a hearty green salad.

SERVES 4 | Prep Time: 5 minutes | Cook Time: 15 minutes

12 ounces whole-wheat medium pasta shells
1½ cups frozen peas
2 tablespoons olive oil
1 tablespoon lemon zest
1 cup ricotta cheese
3 tablespoons finely chopped mint leaves
½ teaspoon ground black pepper
2 tablespoons grated Parmigiano cheese

1. Bring a large pot of well-salted water to a boil. Add pasta and cook until al dente according to package instructions. In the last 2 minutes of pasta cooking, add peas to same pot. Reserve 1½ cups pasta cooking water and then drain pasta and peas.

2. Return pasta and peas to pot and reduce heat to low. Add reserved pasta water, oil, zest, ricotta cheese, mint, and pepper. Mix well 1 minute.

3. Portion pasta into bowls and top with Parmigiano. Serve.

PER SERVING

Calories: 384 · Fat: 15g	
Protein: 16g · Sodium: 276mg	
Fiber: 7g · Carbohydrates: 38g	
Net Carbs: 31g · Sugar: 4g	

······· **BABY FOOD** ·······

This recipe is fine for babies with appropriate chewing skills. Mash the peas if needed to accommodate the baby's level of chewing skills.

Butternut–Black Bean Enchilada Squares GF | EF | NF | CT

This recipe is especially nice in the fall, when farmers' markets are full of cool-looking squash. Instead of rolling each enchilada, we stack the tortillas and cut it like lasagna.

SERVES 8 | Prep Time: 20 minutes | Cook Time: 1 hour

¼ cup extra-virgin olive oil, divided
1¼ cups small diced onion, divided
¾ teaspoon smoked paprika
2 tablespoons plus 2 teaspoons
    Tex-Mex Spice Blend, divided
    (see Chapter 6)
3 cloves garlic, peeled and minced
2½ cups tomato purée
1½ cups water, divided
1½ teaspoons salt, divided
¾ cup roughly chopped cilantro,
    divided
1 cup medium diced red bell pepper
1 (15-ounce) can black beans,
    strained and rinsed
2 cups mashed butternut squash
12 (6"–8") corn tortillas
2 cups grated Cheddar cheese

PER SERVING

Calories: 378 · Fat: 16g	
Protein: 15g · Sodium: 781mg	
Fiber: 11g · Carbohydrates: 43g	
Net Carbs: 32g · Sugar: 8g	

1. **Make the sauce:** Warm 2 tablespoons oil in a medium-large sauté pan over medium heat. Add ¾ cup onions, smoked paprika, and 1 tablespoon plus 1 teaspoon of Tex-Mex Spice Blend and sauté 3 minutes. Add garlic, sauté 30 more seconds, and then add tomato purée, 1 cup water, and ¾ teaspoon salt. Reduce heat to medium-low and cook 25 minutes. Turn off heat and stir in ¼ cup cilantro.

2. **Make the filling:** Warm remaining 2 tablespoons oil in another large sauté pan over medium heat. Add remaining 1 cup onions, remaining 1 tablespoon Tex-Mex Spice Blend, and red pepper. Sauté 5 minutes. Add beans plus ½ cup water and remaining ¾ teaspoon salt. Cook another 7 minutes.

3. Using a potato masher or fork, mash beans while they cook. Stir in squash and cook another 3 minutes. Stir well to combine. Turn off heat and add remaining ½ cup cilantro.

4. Preheat oven to 400°F. **Make the enchiladas:** In a 9" × 13" pan, layer 6 tortillas to cover the bottom of pan. Spread bean-butternut filling evenly over tortillas. Top with remaining 6 tortillas. Pour and spread enchilada sauce evenly over tortillas. Top with cheese.

5. Bake 20 minutes until mixture is warmed through and cheese on top is bubbly and melted. Cut into eight pieces and serve hot.

Miso Soba Bowl   GF | DF | NF | CT

Kids who love noodle soup or instant ramen will love this homemade version. In addition to the suggested toppings, you could also top it with cooked vegetables, meat or fish, tofu, pickled vegetables, or kimchee. Prepare the base and let kids be creative with their own toppings, artistically arranged. If you want to make sure this soup is gluten-free, get soba noodles that are 100 percent buckwheat.

SERVES 4 | Prep Time: 10 minutes | Cook Time: 20 minutes

2 teaspoons toasted sesame oil

2 teaspoons minced fresh ginger

½ cup thinly sliced shiitake mushrooms

1 tablespoon plus 1 teaspoon gluten-free tamari, divided

1 quart vegetable stock

3 tablespoons miso paste

1 (8-ounce) package soba noodles, cooked according to package instructions

4 large eggs, boiled and peeled

1 sheet nori, cut in strips

1 (8-ounce) can bamboo shoots

1 tablespoon Nori Gomasio (see Chapter 6)

······· **BABY FOOD** ·······

As is, this recipe is too salty for babies. But a small spoonful of miso stirred into cooked and mashed egg and vegetables is a great way to enhance flavor and introduce probiotics to babies. Plain rice noodles are also fun finger food for babies.

1. In a medium saucepot over low heat, heat oil. Add ginger and heat until aromatic, about 1 minute.

2. Add mushrooms plus 1 teaspoon tamari and cook another 3 minutes until mushrooms soften.

3. Add stock and remaining tamari to pot. Bring to a boil. Simmer 5 minutes.

4. Put miso paste in a small bowl, add a large ladleful of stock, and mix well with a fork or whisk until paste is evenly mixed into broth. Pour miso mixture back into rest of broth.

5. Divide cooked noodles among four bowls. Pour hot broth over noodles, evenly distributed among bowls.

6. Top each bowl as desired with an egg (cut in half), nori strips, and portion of bamboo and Nori Gomasio.

PER SERVING

Calories: 225 · Fat: 9g · Protein: 15g · Sodium: 1,770mg
Fiber: 2g · Carbohydrates: 21g · Net Carbs: 19g · Sugar: 5g

Lentil Soup   GF | DF | EF | NF

Every family should have a staple lentil soup recipe. It is hearty, comforting, and affordable! This recipe makes enough to feed a family of four, with leftovers. It freezes well or can be refrigerated up to four days. Serve with rice or a slice of whole-wheat bread drizzled with olive oil and Dukkah (see Chapter 6).

SERVES 6 | Prep Time: 10 minutes | Cook Time: 35–45 minutes

3 tablespoons olive oil
1 small onion, peeled and diced small
½ cup diced tomatoes (canned or fresh)
1½ cups French lentils, rinsed
2 teaspoons salt
½ teaspoon ground black pepper
3 medium carrots, diced medium
3 medium stalks celery, diced medium
7 cups water
2 bay leaves
5 cups packed baby spinach
⅓ cup chopped fresh parsley
Juice of ½ medium lemon
2 tablespoons Green Oil (see Chapter 6)

1. In a large pot over medium heat, warm oil. Add onions and sauté about 3 minutes.
2. Add tomatoes, lentils, salt, and pepper. Sauté 2 minutes, stirring frequently.
3. Add carrots, celery, water, and bay leaves. Bring to a boil and then reduce heat to low so soup simmers.
4. Cook about 25 minutes or until lentils are completely tender but not falling apart. (This may take up to 35 minutes depending on lentils.)
5. Add spinach and cook another 3 minutes or until it is fully wilted.
6. Turn off heat. Remove bay leaves and discard them. Stir in parsley and lemon.
7. Serve hot with 1 teaspoon Green Oil drizzled on top.

······· BABY FOOD ·······

This soup makes excellent baby food if you leave out or reduce the salt. Mash or purée further after cooking as needed.

PER SERVING

Calories: 256 · Fat: 9g · Protein: 13g · Sodium: 920mg

Fiber: 12g · Carbohydrates: 32g · Net Carbs: 20g · Sugar: 5g

Chicken Shawarma GF | DF | EF | NF

Your family will love this tasty recipe! Serve with Tomato, Cucumber, and Bulgur Salad (see Chapter 10) and/or inside a warmed pita. The same cooking method can be used for other meats and fish like lamb, turkey cutlets, or fresh mackerel. If you are grilling, you can leave the avocado oil out of this recipe.

SERVES 4 | Prep Time: 5 minutes, plus 4 hours passive (for marinating) | Cook Time: 15 minutes

2 teaspoons Basic Anti-Inflammatory Spice Blend (see Chapter 6)
¾ teaspoon salt
½ teaspoon ground cinnamon
4 boneless, skinless chicken thighs (about 1–1¼ pounds)
1 tablespoon avocado oil (if cooking on stovetop)

PER SERVING

Calories: 242 · Fat: 12g	
Protein: 29g · Sodium: 559mg	
Fiber: 1g · Carbohydrates: 1g	
Net Carbs: 0g · Sugar: 0g	

······· BABY FOOD ·······

After fully cooking, shred a small piece of chicken or purée with breastmilk or formula.

1. In a small bowl, whisk together Basic Anti-Inflammatory Spice Blend, salt, and cinnamon. Rub spice mixture on chicken and allow to marinate in the refrigerator about 4 hours or up to overnight.

2. Chicken may be cooked on the stovetop in a large cast iron or nonstick pan, or it may be grilled. If using a pan, warm oil over medium heat and add chicken to pan.

3. Cook on each side about 6–8 minutes or until chicken is cooked through and opaque at its thickest part and the internal temperature reaches 165°F. If using a grill, leave out oil and grill for 6–8 minutes per side until chicken is cooked through.

4. Slice chicken into ¼" slices and serve.

Tempeh Coconut Curry GF | DF | EF | NF

Use this recipe as a basic template and then add or substitute with odds and ends from the refrigerator. To make it even quicker, your favorite prepared curry paste can replace the ginger, garlic, scallions, lime zest, and red chili flakes. Extra-firm tofu, chicken, or shrimp work well in place of tempeh. Serve with sticky (sushi) rice or rice noodles.

SERVES 4 | Prep Time: 20 minutes | Cook Time: 35 minutes

2½ tablespoons coconut oil, divided
1 (2") piece fresh ginger, peeled and minced
6 cloves garlic, peeled and minced
4 medium scallions, cut into thin rounds
1 medium lime, zested
1 teaspoon red chili flakes
1 medium green bell pepper, cut into ½" slices
8 ounces shiitake mushrooms, sliced
2 medium carrots, diced medium
1 (15-ounce) can unsweetened coconut milk
2½ cups vegetable stock
1 teaspoon salt, divided
½ teaspoon ground black pepper
1 teaspoon ground turmeric
2 tablespoons gluten-free tamari
1 tablespoon lime juice
8 ounces tempeh, cut in ½" cubes
2½ cups packed baby spinach

1. In a large pot over medium heat, warm 1 tablespoon oil. Add ginger, garlic, scallions, lime zest, and chili flakes. Sauté about 2 minutes or until fragrant.
2. Add bell pepper, mushrooms, and carrots. Cook about 5 minutes or until vegetables begin to soften.
3. Add milk and stock. Add ¾ teaspoon salt, black pepper, turmeric, tamari, and lime juice. Bring to a simmer. Cook about 20 minutes or until carrots are tender.
4. In the meantime, heat remaining 1½ tablespoons oil in a large sauté pan over medium heat.
5. Add tempeh and ¼ teaspoon salt. Sauté until golden brown on all sides, about 4–5 minutes.
6. Add spinach and tempeh to pot with vegetables. Cook another 3 minutes or until spinach is wilted. Serve hot!

PER SERVING

Calories: 500	*Fat: 38g*	*Protein: 18g*	*Sodium: 1,689mg*
Fiber: 6g	*Carbohydrates: 26g*	*Net Carbs: 20g*	
Sugar: 8g			

Creamy Chicken Soup GF | NF

This recipe is inspired by avgolemono, a Greek chicken soup that is made creamy by stirring in an egg, cheese, and lemon at the end. It's like a little bit of kitchen magic, which kids will love watching and helping with. To make it dairy- and egg-free, simply leave out this step, and it's still a delicious chicken vegetable soup.

SERVES 8 | Prep Time: 15 minutes | Cook Time: 50 minutes

2 tablespoons extra-virgin olive oil

1 pound bone-in chicken thighs
    or legs

2 teaspoons salt, divided

1 teaspoon ground black pepper

½ teaspoon turmeric

2 medium stalks celery, diced small

1 medium onion, peeled and diced
    small

6 cups water

1 (8-ounce) bag baby spinach

2 large eggs

⅓ cup fresh lemon juice

2 tablespoons grated pecorino
    cheese

2 tablespoons chopped parsley

2 tablespoons chopped dill

· · · · · · BABY FOOD · · · · · · ·

Purée a portion of the soup after cooking or serve "deconstructed" portions of shredded chicken and soft, mashed vegetables.

· ·

1. In a large, heavy-bottomed soup pot over medium heat, heat oil. Season chicken with 1 teaspoon salt, pepper, and turmeric. Add chicken to pot and brown on both sides, about 3 minutes per side.

2. Add celery and onion and sauté about 10 more minutes with remaining 1 teaspoon salt.

3. Add water. Bring to a boil and then reduce to a simmer. Cook 30 minutes.

4. Add spinach and cook another 5 minutes. Then turn off heat. Remove chicken, shred it, and return to pot.

5. In a medium bowl, mix eggs, lemon juice, and pecorino.

6. While whisking constantly, *slowly* drizzle a full ladle of hot soup stock into egg mixture to temper it. (This is so it doesn't turn to scrambled eggs when it hits hot soup.) Then *slowly* drizzle egg mixture into soup pot, whisking constantly. Soup will thicken and become creamy.

7. Ladle soup into bowls, sprinkle with chopped parsley and dill, and serve hot.

PER SERVING

Calories: 143 · Fat: 8g · Protein: 13g · Sodium: 699mg

Fiber: 1g · Carbohydrates: 4g · Net Carbs: 3g · Sugar: 1g

Fish Sticks GF | DF

This is a great recipe to habituate kids to eating fish! We use pollock here, but you could easily substitute another white fish such as cod, flounder, or a sustainably farmed tilapia. Use Flax Eggs (see Chapter 6) to accommodate allergies if needed.

SERVES 4 | Prep Time: 8 minutes | Cook Time: 8 minutes

1 pound pollock fillet
1¼ cups Nut Crumbs (see
  Chapter 6)
1 large egg
¼ teaspoon salt
¼ cup avocado oil
1 medium lemon, cut into 4
  wedges

PER SERVING
(Serving size: 2 fish sticks)

Calories: 370 · Fat: 31g	
Protein: 21g · Sodium: 659mg	
Fiber: 3g · Carbohydrates: 12g	
Net Carbs: 9g · Sugar: 1g	

······· BABY FOOD ·······

After cooking, mash or cut the fish into appropriately sized pieces to accommodate your baby's level of chewing skills.

1. Cut pollock into sticks that are approximately 4" × 1½".

2. Place Nut Crumbs in a medium shallow bowl. In a separate medium shallow bowl, beat together egg and salt.

3. In a medium frying pan over medium heat, heat oil 30 seconds. Keep heat low enough so oil does not smoke.

4. Working with one fish stick at a time, dip fish first in egg batter, letting excess egg drip off, and then coat it with nut mixture, patting mixture into fish firmly so it sticks. Repeat with remaining fish.

5. Put fish sticks in pan in one layer. Make sure fish sticks are not too tightly packed into pan. Work in two batches if necessary.

6. Cook fish sticks until undersides are browned and crispy, about 3–4 minutes. Then turn over and cook 3–4 minutes on other side. Fish is done when both sides are crispy and inside is opaque and flakes easily when a fork is put through it.

7. Serve hot with lemon wedges.

Meatball and Escarole Soup NF | CT

This is a satisfying one-pot meal that can feed a family of four with significant leftovers that you can freeze or save for later in the week. Make it gluten-free by substituting leftover rice or almond meal for the bread crumbs, and make it dairy-free by leaving out the cheese and egg and instead using a Flax Egg (see Chapter 6).

SERVES 8 | Prep Time: 30 minutes | Cook Time: 30 minutes

1 (15-ounce) can chickpeas, drained

16 ounces ground turkey

3 cloves garlic, peeled and minced

⅔ cup chopped fresh parsley, divided

3 tablespoons bread crumbs

6 tablespoons grated pecorino cheese, divided

1 large egg

3 tablespoons extra-virgin olive oil

1 cup medium diced celery

2 cups medium diced carrots

2 cups medium diced red potatoes

1¼ teaspoons salt

8 cups water

4 cups chopped escarole

PER SERVING

Calories: 256 · Fat: 12g

Protein: 16g · Sodium: 619mg

Fiber: 5g · Carbohydrates: 20g

Net Carbs: 15g · Sugar: 4g

1. Mash chickpeas to form a smooth paste, either with a potato masher or in a food processor.

2. In a large bowl, combine chickpeas, turkey, garlic, ⅓ cup parsley, bread crumbs, 3 tablespoons pecorino, and egg. Mix well using clean hands into a uniform consistency.

3. Fill a small bowl with warm water and set it near turkey mixture. Make meatballs by pinching off a piece of mixture and rolling it between your palms to form a 1" ball. Place them on a plate while working. In between meatballs, dip your hands in the water bowl to keep your hands clean and wet—this will make the process less sticky! The mixture will yield about 30 meatballs.

4. In a large pot over medium heat, warm oil. Then add celery and carrots. Cook 5 minutes.

5. Add potatoes and salt. Cook another 5 minutes. Add water and bring to a boil.

6. Add meatballs, dropping them one by one into soup. Cook 5 minutes.

7. Reduce to a low boil, add escarole, and cook another 15 minutes.

8. Serve hot, garnished with remaining parsley and pecorino.

CHAPTER 10

Sides

Variety is key to enjoying food and eating the anti-inflammatory way. A variety of vegetable- and whole-grain-forward dishes make for a colorful table, a rich array of leftovers, and something for everyone. While the recipes in this chapter make excellent accompaniments to protein-rich foods like fish, chicken, or tofu, they certainly don't need to be relegated to the "sides" of the plate. They can easily turn into main dinner items with a bit of rounding out. Combine the Cheesy Grits with collards and add a fried egg. Cauliflower Rice and Beans makes a complete meal with the Pico de Gallo and Guacamole in Chapter 11. Or turn the Grilled Whole-Wheat Flatbread into a pizza by adding a few toppings and serve with a hearty green salad.

The simplest side dish that you won't see much of here is green salad. That's not because we don't love them, but rather because they are so easy they don't need recipes. Combine lettuce or mixed greens with whatever vegetables, fruits, and nuts you happen to have around. Top them with one of the dressings in Chapter 6, and you've just added a hearty dose of anti-inflammatory phytochemicals to your meal.

Cauliflower Rice and Beans GF | DF | EF | NF

Cauliflower rice can be found in the produce or freezer section of most grocery stores. Or make it at home by placing cauliflower florets in a food processor and pulsing until it is minced and resembles rice. Alternately, grate the cauliflower on a box grater for the same effect. This dish is delicious topped with Pico de Gallo (see Chapter 11) and makes a nice filling for a burrito with avocado.

SERVES 4 | Prep Time: 15 minutes | Cook Time: 20 minutes

2 tablespoons olive oil
2 cloves garlic, peeled and minced
½ teaspoon ground coriander
½ teaspoon ground cumin
1 pound (about 4 cups) cauli-
    flower rice
½ teaspoon salt
½ teaspoon ground black pepper
1 (15½-ounce) can black beans,
    drained and rinsed
2 tablespoons chopped cilantro
¼ cup lime juice

1. In a large sauté pan over medium-low heat, combine oil, garlic, coriander, and cumin. Sauté 30 seconds, taking care not to brown garlic.

2. Add rice and sauté 10–15 minutes until cauliflower is tender. Season with salt and pepper.

3. Add beans, cilantro, and lime juice. Cook another 5 minutes until beans are warmed through.

PER SERVING

Calories: 189 · Fat: 7g
Protein: 9g · Sodium: 556mg
Fiber: 10g · Carbohydrates: 25g
Net Carbs: 15g · Sugar: 3g

· · · · · · · BABY FOOD · · · · · · ·

Once this dish is cooked, mash well so the beans are no longer whole, or purée the whole thing with breastmilk or formula.

Garlicky Mashed Potatoes and Parsnips GF | EF | NF

This is a good way to introduce the flavor of a vegetable that may be new for kids (parsnips) with a well-loved one (potatoes). For an extra anti-inflammatory kick, add a teaspoon of the Basic Anti-Inflammatory Spice Blend (see Chapter 6).

Phytonutrient focus: Garlic has anticancer properties, due in large part to its sulfur compounds, and it protects the health of your arteries and heart. It is also strongly anti-microbial and can help your body fight against colds, bacteria, and infections. Long story short—a clove of garlic a day keeps the bad stuff away!

SERVES 4 | Prep Time: 10 minutes | Cook Time: 50 minutes

1 whole bulb garlic, stem removed
2 tablespoons extra-virgin olive oil
3 large red potatoes, peeled and chopped
2 medium parsnips, peeled and chopped
2 tablespoons butter
½ cup whole milk
1 teaspoon salt

······ BABY FOOD ·······

This makes a great base to add in greens, such as spinach or kale.

1. Preheat oven to 350°F.
2. Using a sharp knife, cut the top off garlic bulb (about ¼" from the top) so insides of individual cloves are just exposed. Place garlic on a piece of tin foil large enough to cover it. Drizzle top of bulb with oil. Wrap it in foil and roast about 20 minutes or until garlic is soft. Remove from oven and cool.
3. In a large pot, add potatoes and parsnips and cover with cold water. Place pot on stove and bring to a boil. Then reduce to a simmer. Cook about 30 minutes or until potatoes and parsnips are fork-tender.
4. Drain potatoes and parsnips and return to pot. Add butter, milk, and salt. Carefully squeeze roasted garlic out of its skin. Add to pot.
5. Using a potato masher, mash until smooth (or to desired texture). Serve.

PER SERVING

Calories: 357	*Fat: 13g*	*Protein: 6g*	*Sodium: 610mg*
Fiber: 6g	*Carbohydrates: 55g*	*Net Carbs: 49g*	*Sugar: 5g*

Greek Green Beans GF | EF | NF

The long, slow cooking process in this recipe draws out the sweetness of the beans. You can use either fresh or frozen green beans for this recipe. Eliminate the feta to make it dairy-free.

Phytonutrient focus: Onions, a humble bulb at the base of so many recipes, are one of the richest sources of dietary flavonoids, including one named quercetin, which has strong anti-inflammatory and immune-modulating properties. You can find quercetin in pill form, but as with all supplements, it's not nearly as effective isolated as it is in the context of the whole food and whole diet.

SERVES 6 | Prep Time: 10 minutes | Cook Time: 1 hour

3 tablespoons olive oil

1 large onion, peeled and sliced thin

2 cloves garlic, peeled and minced

1 (15-ounce) can diced tomatoes

1 teaspoon salt

1½ pounds green beans, ends trimmed and cut in 3" pieces

2 cups water

½ cup chopped fresh parsley leaves

½ cup crumbled feta cheese

······ BABY FOOD ······

This dish is great for babies because the beans are quite soft. Skip the feta. Mash/cut in very small pieces or purée with breastmilk or formula.

1. In a large sauté pan over medium heat, heat oil 30 seconds. Add onions and cook 5 minutes.

2. Add garlic and cook 30 seconds. Then add tomatoes and salt and cook 5–7 minutes, smashing some of the tomato pieces with a wooden spoon to make it saucy.

3. Add green beans and water. Stir, cover with a lid, and let cook 15 minutes.

4. Remove lid and cook another 20–30 minutes until liquid is mostly evaporated and beans are very tender. Remove from heat and stir in parsley.

5. Serve with feta cheese sprinkled on top.

PER SERVING

Calories: 162 · Fat: 9g · Protein: 5g · Sodium: 635mg

Fiber: 5g · Carbohydrates: 16g · Net Carbs: 11g · Sugar: 5g

Zucchini and Corn Fritters GF

These fritters are especially delicious in summer when zucchini and corn are in abundance. You can also use frozen and then thawed corn kernels if you don't have fresh. For the dipping sauce, if you like a less spicy option, reduce or omit the sriracha or substitute with pesto. Or, to make it dairy-free, eliminate the dipping sauce.

SERVES 4 | Prep Time: 20 minutes | Cook Time: 20 minutes

¼ cup sriracha sauce

1 cup plain, whole milk Greek
    yogurt

1 cup shredded zucchini

1 cup chickpeas, mashed well

1 cup fresh corn kernels

3 large eggs, whisked

1 cup almond meal

¼ cup chopped fresh parsley

1 teaspoon salt

½ teaspoon ground black pepper

½ teaspoon turmeric

¼ cup avocado oil, divided

1. In a small bowl, whisk together sriracha and yogurt. Set aside to serve with fritters.

2. In a large bowl, combine zucchini, chickpeas, corn, eggs, almond meal, parsley, salt, pepper, and turmeric.

3. In a medium sauté pan over medium heat, heat 1 tablespoon oil, taking care not to let it smoke. Scoop about 2 tablespoons batter for each fritter onto pan into round disks.

4. Cook on both sides for about 3 minutes or until golden brown. Repeat with remaining batter, adding oil as necessary.

5. Serve fritters hot or at room temperature with dipping sauce.

PER SERVING

Calories: 467 · Fat: 31g

Protein: 20g · Sodium: 1,044mg

Fiber: 7g · Carbohydrates: 27g

Net Carbs: 20g · Sugar: 11g

· · · · · · · BABY FOOD · · · · · · ·

These fritters make good finger food, minus the corn, which can be a choking hazard. Serve with plain yogurt rather than the sriracha yogurt.

Coconut Kale GF | DF | EF | NF

This creamy, flavorful preparation works well with any leafy greens, like collards, mustard greens, or Swiss chard. You can adjust the spice level to your taste or leave the Basic Anti-Inflammatory Spice Blend out altogether.

Phytonutrient focus: Coconuts have many medicinal properties, including antimicrobial, antioxidant, and skin protective (try coconut oil as skin cream!). The fats in coconut oil are mainly medium-chained saturated fats, which you can think of as "sometimes" fats. Overall, coconut products are best eaten as they have been traditionally—in moderation in the context of whole, healthy diets.

SERVES 4 | Prep Time: 10 minutes | Cook Time: 13 minutes

1 tablespoon coconut oil

1 small onion, peeled and diced small

1 tablespoon Basic Anti-Inflammatory Spice Blend (see Chapter 6)

2 cloves garlic, peeled and minced

1 (½") piece fresh ginger, peeled and minced

1 bunch kale, rinsed, hard stems removed and coarsely chopped

1 cup canned unsweetened coconut milk

½ cup water

¼ teaspoon salt

1. In a medium skillet, melt oil over medium heat. Add onions and Basic Anti-Inflammatory Spice Blend and sauté 3 minutes.

2. Add garlic and ginger and sauté another 30 seconds until aromatic.

3. Add kale, milk, water, and salt. Stir to combine.

4. Once kale wilts down a bit (after about 1 minute), place a lid on pan, lower heat to a simmer, and cook about 10 minutes. Check on greens every few minutes to make sure they are not drying out. If they are, add a few tablespoons of water to moisten. Remove from heat when kale is very tender. Serve immediately.

······· BABY FOOD ·······

This is a great recipe for babies, removing the salt. Purée it with formula or breastmilk or chop the kale very small after it's cooked. This also makes a nice addition to mashed potatoes and parsnips.

PER SERVING

Calories: 209 · Fat: 17g · Protein: 4g · Sodium: 408mg

Fiber: 4g · Carbohydrates: 12g · Net Carbs: 8g · Sugar: 4g

Braised Collard Greens GF | DF | EF | NF

This dish is a really flavorful, and much faster, version of traditional southern collard greens.

Phytonutrient focus: Collards are a cruciferous vegetable in the Brassica family. Vegetables in this family (like kale, mustard greens, cauliflower, broccoli, and cabbage) have a group of sulfur-containing phytochemicals called glucosinolates, which many studies link with a reduction in the risk of multiple kinds of cancer. These compounds work in concert with many others that are anti-inflammatory and heart protective. Among the already wonderful world of vegetables, Brassicas are superstars.

SERVES 4 | Prep Time: 10 minutes | Cook Time: 40 minutes

2 tablespoons extra-virgin olive oil
1 cup small diced yellow onion
2 cloves garlic, peeled and minced
1 bunch collard greens, hard stems removed and cut into 1" strips (about 6 packed cups)
1½ cups water
3 tablespoons apple cider vinegar
¼ teaspoon salt
¼ teaspoon ground black pepper
1 teaspoon ground coriander
1 tablespoon pure maple syrup
¼ teaspoon red pepper flakes

1. In a large sauté pan over low heat, warm oil. Add onions and cook 7 minutes until they are tender and transparent.

2. Add garlic and sauté 30 seconds, just until fragrant.

3. Add collards and water to pan. After 1 minute, once greens have wilted down a bit, add remaining ingredients to pan.

4. Cover with a lid and cook 30 minutes. Check on greens every 5 minutes. If they look dry, add water, 1 cup at a time. It's important that they are cooking in liquid throughout. Serve hot.

· · · · · · BABY FOOD · · · · · ·

This is a great recipe for babies, eliminating the salt. Purée it with formula or breastmilk or chop it very small after it's fully cooked. This also makes a nice addition to mashed potatoes and parsnips.

PER SERVING

Calories: 110 · Fat: 7g · Protein: 2g · Sodium: 157mg

Fiber: 3g · Carbohydrates: 11g · Net Carbs: 8g · Sugar: 5g

Sweet Spiced Delicata Squash GF | DF | EF

Make this recipe with any squash, including butternut, acorn, or pumpkin. Delicata squash is especially easy to work with and doesn't need to be peeled. Pistachios (or any nut) are a great garnish, but you can eliminate them to accommodate allergies.

SERVES 6 | Prep Time: 15 minutes | Cook Time: 35 minutes

3 pounds delicata squash (2–3 squash, depending on size)
3 tablespoons extra-virgin olive oil
2 tablespoons pure maple syrup
1 teaspoon salt
1 teaspoon Sweet Spice Blend (see Chapter 6)
¼ teaspoon ground nutmeg
1½ teaspoons lemon juice
3 tablespoons roughly chopped pistachios

1. Preheat oven to 350°F.
2. Cut squash lengthwise and remove and discard seeds. Cut into ½"-thick half-moons.
3. Place squash on a baking sheet and drizzle with oil and maple syrup. Toss with salt, Sweet Spice Blend, and nutmeg. Make sure squash is evenly coated with all ingredients.
4. Bake about 35 minutes until squash is soft inside and lightly browned and caramelized on outside.
5. Serve sprinkled with lemon juice and nuts.

PER SERVING

Calories: 179 · Fat: 8g	
Protein: 5g · Sodium: 388mg	
Fiber: 5g · Carbohydrates: 26g	
Net Carbs: 21g · Sugar: 12g	

· · · · · · · BABY FOOD · · · · · · ·

If making this dish for babies, peel the squash, either before or after baking, and eliminate salt and pistachios, as they could be a choking hazard. Serve as a finger food or mashed.

Fennel Slaw GF | DF | EF | NF

This recipe is great for little hands to help with when it's time to massage the cabbage, which helps break down the cabbage and soften it. It's a delicious accompaniment to chicken tenders or fish tacos.

SERVES 6 | Prep Time: 25 minutes | Cook Time: n/a

2 cups shredded red cabbage
1 teaspoon salt, divided
1 tablespoon orange juice
2 tablespoons lime juice
2 teaspoons rice wine vinegar
3 tablespoons extra-virgin olive oil
1 tablespoon honey
1 medium carrot, grated (about ½ cup)
1 medium bulb fennel, finely sliced (about 1 cup)
¼ cup chopped fresh cilantro
½ cup toasted pumpkin seeds

1. In a large bowl, place cabbage and ½ teaspoon salt. Massage with your hands for 3–4 minutes. Leave to rest.
2. In a small bowl, whisk orange juice, lime juice, vinegar, oil, honey, and remaining salt.
3. To the bowl with cabbage, add carrots, fennel, cilantro, pumpkin seeds, and dressing. Mix well. Serve.

PER SERVING

Calories: 144 · Fat: 11g · Protein: 4g · Sodium: 410mg
Fiber: 2g · Carbohydrates: 9g · Net Carbs: 7g · Sugar: 5g

· · · · · · BABY FOOD · · · · · · ·

The raw vegetables in this recipe are challenging to chew and not appropriate for babies. Instead, cook cabbage, carrots, and fennel in olive oil and a little water until they are quite soft. Add cilantro and then mash or purée.

· ·

Sweet Pickled Shiitake and Ginger GF | DF | EF | NF

This is a super tasty way to prepare shiitake mushrooms that kids will love. It makes a great condiment for rice dishes, noodles, and even sandwiches. Once you've eaten the mushrooms, use the pickling liquid to season other foods, such as to marinate fish, in salad dressings, or add to stir-fry vegetables.

Phytonutrient focus: Shiitake are a delicious mushroom with strong medicinal properties. They are high in eritadenine, which has cholesterol-lowering and heart-protective properties. The polysaccharides, especially beta-glucan, can improve immune function. Along with other medicinal mushrooms, they are also used as an effective addition to cancer therapies.

SERVES 8 | Prep Time: 10 minutes, plus 30 minutes passive | Cook Time: 15 minutes

2 cups dried shiitake mushroom caps (about 12 large caps)
¼ cup gluten-free tamari
¼ cup brown rice vinegar
2 tablespoons pure maple syrup
1 (2") piece fresh ginger, peeled and cut into thin slices

······· BABY FOOD ·······

These pickled shiitake can be hard for babies to chew. Instead, sauté fresh shiitake mushrooms in olive oil for 10 minutes. Cut finely or purée with breastmilk or formula.

1. Put mushrooms in a small saucepan and cover with boiling water. Let them soak about 30 minutes. Drain mushrooms, reserving 1 cup soaking liquid.
2. Slice rehydrated mushrooms into ¼" slices.
3. Return mushrooms and reserved soaking liquid to saucepan and add tamari, vinegar, maple syrup, and ginger. Simmer 15 minutes over low heat.
4. Remove from heat and cool to room temperature. Store in an airtight container (along with liquid). Eat immediately or keep refrigerated up to two weeks.

PER SERVING

Calories: 19 · Fat: 0g · Protein: 1g · Sodium: 101mg
Fiber: 1g · Carbohydrates: 5g · Net Carbs: 4g · Sugar: 1g

Roasted Cauliflower with Dukkah GF | DF | EF

If you haven't introduced roasted cauliflower to your kids yet (and you're skeptical), it's a must! Roasting vegetables is one of the easiest ways to make them kid friendly. This preparation adds a Middle Eastern flair. Note that you can make this recipe with any vegetable that lends itself to roasting, like broccoli, beets, squash, or sweet potatoes. Eliminate the Dukkah to make it nut-free.

SERVES 6 | Prep Time: 10 minutes | Cook Time: 30–40 minutes

1 medium head cauliflower, cut into bite-sized (2") florets
3 tablespoons extra-virgin olive oil
½ teaspoon salt
2½ tablespoons Lemon-Tahini Dressing (see Chapter 6)
2 tablespoons Dukkah (see Chapter 6)

1. Preheat oven to 350°F.
2. On a baking sheet, combine cauliflower, oil, and salt and roast for 30–40 minutes until outside is browned and crisp and inside is tender. Remove from heat onto a serving platter.
3. Spoon Lemon-Tahini Dressing over cauliflower and sprinkle with Dukkah. Serve hot or at room temperature.

PER SERVING

Calories: 123 · Fat: 10g	
Protein: 3g · Sodium: 297mg	
Fiber: 3g · Carbohydrates: 8g	
Net Carbs: 5g · Sugar: 3g	

· · · · · · BABY FOOD · · · · · · ·

Serve roasted cauliflower with a bit of Lemon-Tahini Dressing, but eliminate the Dukkah, which contains choking hazards. The cauliflower and tahini can be a finger food or mashed/puréed with breastmilk or formula.

Quick Vegetable Pickles GF | DF | EF | NF | CT

Pickles are usually a production, but these quick pickles take no time at all. If you don't have mustard seeds, feel free to use premixed pickling spice. This recipe is for a modest batch size, but could be easily doubled, quadrupled, or more. Pickles will keep up to four weeks in the refrigerator and will get tastier as time goes on.

SERVES 4 | Prep Time: 15 minutes, plus 1 hour passive | Cook Time: 5 minutes

½ cup cucumber slices
½ cup onion slices
½ cup carrot slices
½ cup red bell pepper strips
½ cup apple cider vinegar
½ cup water
1½ teaspoons salt
2 teaspoons mustard seeds

1. Pack cut vegetables tightly into a Mason jar.
2. In a small saucepan over high heat, combine vinegar, water, salt, and mustard seeds. Bring to a boil.
3. Pour hot liquid over vegetables. Cap jar and let steep at least 1 hour at room temperature. If not using the same day, put in refrigerator until ready to serve.

PER SERVING
Calories: 18 · Fat: 0g
Protein: 1g · Sodium: 98mg
Fiber: 1g · Carbohydrates: 4g
Net Carbs: 3g · Sugar: 2g

········· BABY FOOD ·······

These pickled vegetables are too crunchy for babies. Instead, sauté the vegetables in olive oil. Cut finely or purée with breast-milk or formula.

Tomato, Cucumber, and Bulgur Salad DF | EF | NF

This is a great summer side dish and pairs especially well with the Chicken Shawarma in Chapter 9. To make it gluten-free, use quinoa instead of bulgur.

SERVES 4 | Prep Time: 15 minutes | Cook Time: 10 minutes

½ cup bulgur

1½ cups water

¾ teaspoon salt, divided

2 tablespoons lemon juice

3 tablespoons extra-virgin olive oil

1 cup medium diced tomato

1 cup medium diced cucumber

⅓ cup finely chopped fresh parsley

······· BABY FOOD ·······

Bulgur prepared this way can be a challenging texture for babies, and the raw vegetables can be choking hazards. Instead, make bulgur porridge by cooking bulgur for 20 minutes in twice as much water, and then blending with breastmilk, formula, or yogurt. Add mashed fruit or vegetables as desired.

1. In a small saucepan over medium-high heat, combine bulgur, water, and ¼ teaspoon salt. Bring to a boil. Then cover, reduce heat to simmer, and cook 10 minutes. Turn off heat and let sit, covered, another 5 minutes. Drain off any excess liquid, fluff bulgur with a fork, and place in a serving bowl, letting it come to room temperature while preparing rest of salad.

2. In a small bowl, whisk together lemon juice, oil, and remaining ½ teaspoon salt.

3. Add tomato, cucumber, and parsley to the bowl with bulgur. Add dressing, toss well to combine, and serve.

PER SERVING

Calories: 161 · Fat: 10g · Protein: 3g · Sodium: 371mg

Fiber: 4g · Carbohydrates: 16g · Net Carbs: 12g · Sugar: 2g

Mushroom Barley Bake EF | NF

This indulgent barley bake is risotto-like in texture but easier to cook (just throw it in the oven once begun) and uses barley instead of white rice. Use a store-bought vegetable stock or even water if you don't have homemade stock on hand. For some added protein, add cooked cannellini beans (and a bit more liquid).

SERVES 4 | Prep Time: 10 minutes | Cook Time: 1 hour

2 tablespoons olive oil
½ cup minced onion
2 cloves garlic, peeled and minced
2 cups sliced cremini mushrooms
2 cups sliced shiitake mushrooms
3 cups Vegetable Stock
    (see Chapter 6)
¾ teaspoon salt
1 cup pearl barley
3 tablespoons grated Parmesan
    cheese, divided
2 tablespoons plain, whole milk
    yogurt
1 tablespoon Green Oil
    (see Chapter 6)

1. Preheat oven to 400°F.
2. In a medium saucepan over medium-high heat, heat oil. Add onion and garlic and sauté 1–2 minutes until fragrant. Add mushrooms and cook down until juices start to release and they just start to get soft, about 5 minutes.
3. Add Vegetable Stock and salt and bring to a boil.
4. Meanwhile, grease an 8"-square or round baking dish and add barley and 2 tablespoons Parmesan.
5. Once mushroom mixture has come to a boil, pour it over barley mixture and stir. Cover and bake 50 minutes until barley is cooked through. Check halfway through cooking time. If mixture needs more liquid, add ½ cup of water at a time.
6. Remove from oven and stir in remainder of Parmesan, yogurt, and Green Oil. Serve hot.

······· BABY FOOD ·······

This is a nice recipe for babies with adequate chewing skills. For some, the chewy texture of barley may still be challenging, so purée after cooking, thinning with formula, breastmilk, or yogurt if needed.

PER SERVING

Calories: 324 · Fat: 11g · Protein: 9g · Sodium: 751mg
Fiber: 10g · Carbohydrates: 48g · Net Carbs: 38g · Sugar: 4g

Cheesy Grits GF | EF | NF

These comforting, creamy grits pair nicely with the Fish Sticks in Chapter 9 and Braised Collard Greens (see recipe in this chapter). They also make a hearty breakfast in the winter, accompanied by a simple fried egg.

SERVES 4 | Prep Time: 5 minutes | Cook Time: 20 minutes

¾ cup water
⅔ cup whole milk
¼ teaspoon salt
⅔ cup old-fashioned corn grits
1 tablespoon butter, cut into pieces
2 ounces grated Cheddar cheese

PER SERVING

Calories: 203 · Fat: 8g
Protein: 7g · Sodium: 254mg
Fiber: 1g · Carbohydrates: 23g
Net Carbs: 22g · Sugar: 2g

1. In a medium pot over medium-high heat, bring water, milk, and salt to a boil. Using a whisk, slowly stir grits into boiling water mixture. Stir continuously until grits are well mixed.

2. Bring back to a boil, then cover with a lid and reduce heat to low. Cook about 15 minutes, stirring occasionally until water has absorbed and grits have thickened.

3. Add butter and cheese. Stir until cheese is melted. Remove from heat and serve immediately.

······· BABY FOOD ·······

These grits make a great baby food, minus the salt. Combine with mashed vegetables or beans.

Grilled Whole-Wheat Flatbread DF | EF | NF | CT

Flatbreads are super fun to make with kids and easier to master than most breads. You can also use this dough for a pizza crust.

SERVES 8 | Prep Time: 15 minutes, plus 1 hour, 15–30 minutes for rising | Cook Time: 20 minutes

2 cups whole-wheat flour
1 cup unbleached, all-purpose flour, plus up to ½ cup for dusting and kneading
1½ teaspoons instant yeast
¾ teaspoon salt
1¼ cups warm water, plus 1–2 tablespoons if needed
3 tablespoons extra-virgin olive oil, divided
½ teaspoon sea salt
1 teaspoon dried oregano

PER SERVING

(Serving size: 1 flatbread)

Calories: 206 · Fat: 6g	
Protein: 6g · Sodium: 316mg	
Fiber: 4g · Carbohydrates: 34g	
Net Carbs: 34g · Sugar: 0g	

· · · · · · BABY FOOD · · · · · · ·

Babies with adequate chewing skills will very much enjoy chewing on a piece of this flatbread! Leave out the salt and oregano at the end, but do add the olive oil.

1. In a large bowl, combine flours, yeast, and salt. Add 1¼ cups water and mix well. If needed add 1 tablespoon water at a time until all flour has been absorbed. Then, with clean, well-floured hands, lightly knead dough to bring it together into a ball.

2. Place dough in a large bowl oiled with 1 teaspoon oil. Cover and put in a warm place. Let it rise 1 hour.

3. Transfer risen dough to a cutting board that is well dusted with flour. Knead a couple of times to bring it into a ball. (Note: If using for pizza dough, simply roll it out to the size of your pan and add your toppings.)

4. Cut dough in half, then into four pieces, then eight. Roll each piece into a small ball.

5. Sprinkle a baking sheet with flour and transfer dough balls to it. Put in a warm place for 15–30 minutes.

6. Working one ball at a time on a well-floured board, roll balls with a rolling pin until dough is stretched to a (rough) circle about 8" in diameter.

7. Heat a medium cast iron pan over medium-high heat. DON'T oil it.

8. Once pan is very hot, transfer one flatbread to it. Flip it after 2–3 minutes, when you see underside has a lightly golden color. Cook on other side 2–3 minutes. Repeat with remaining flatbreads.

9. Once out of the pan, brush flatbreads with remaining oil and sprinkle with sea salt and oregano. Serve hot!

CHAPTER 11

Snacks

In this chapter, you will find a fun variety of snack foods. All of these recipes are fantastic starters to get kids involved in cooking. Of course, not every snack needs to be a homemade affair. While most snack foods like chips and sweets are ultra-processed, there are plenty of ready-made snacks that are in line with the anti-inflammatory way. When you don't have time to make the delicious recipes in this chapter, try some of these snack ideas (and put them in easy-to-see places in the refrigerator so kids reach for them first):

- Whole-wheat toast with almond butter and jam, Tahini Maple Syrup (see Chapter 6), or ricotta and honey
- Apple, pear, or banana slices dipped in yogurt or nut butter
- Frozen mango cubes, cherries, or pineapple cubes
- Granola, fruit, and plain yogurt parfait
- Carrots and celery sticks with hummus
- Half a baked sweet potato with almond butter and cacao nibs
- Grapes and cheese cubes
- A hard-boiled egg (sprinkled with the Dukkah in Chapter 6!)

Healthy snacks can be helpful in regulating kids' blood sugar and mood. But overall, remember to keep them to a minimum to promote appetite at mealtimes.

Homemade Pita Chips   DF | EF | NF | CT

These baked chips are fast, easy, and make a fun kids' cooking activity. Use the same recipe to make tortilla chips; just substitute eight corn tortillas for the pita (which also makes it gluten-free). Finally, customize the chips by using one of our other spice blends or other seeds, such as poppy. Serve these with any of the dips in this chapter.

SERVES 5 | Prep Time: 7 minutes | Cook Time: 8–10 minutes

5 (6") whole-wheat pita breads
2 tablespoons extra-virgin olive oil
½ teaspoon salt
1 teaspoon Tex-Mex Spice Blend (see Chapter 6)
1 teaspoon sesame seeds

PER SERVING

(Serving size: 8 chips)

Calories: 222 · Fat: 7g

Protein: 6g · Sodium: 516mg

Fiber: 5g · Carbohydrates: 36g

Net Carbs: 31g · Sugar: 1g

· · · · · · · BABY FOOD · · · · · · ·

Soft pita bread is a better choice for babies than these chips.

1. Preheat oven to 350°F.

2. With a pastry brush, lightly coat each pita with oil (alternately, kids can "paint" them with their fingertip). Cut pitas into eight wedges (like a pizza pie).

3. Place chips in a single layer on a baking sheet. Sprinkle evenly with salt, Tex-Mex Spice Blend, and sesame seeds.

4. Bake 8–10 minutes or until very lightly brown and crispy. They will crisp more as they cool.

Blueberry-Hazelnut Bars GF | DF | EF | CT

These bars make a great grab-and-go breakfast or snack. If you don't have blueberries on hand, try other dried fruits, such as raisins, cranberries, or cherries. Likewise, hazelnuts can be substituted with almonds or walnuts. The bars will keep in an airtight container at room temperature for two to three days...though they usually disappear more quickly than that!

YIELDS 16 BARS | Prep Time: 15 minutes | Cook Time: 25–30 minutes

3 medium very ripe bananas, mashed
¼ cup melted coconut oil
1 tablespoon pure maple syrup
1 teaspoon vanilla extract
1½ cups rolled oats (not instant)
1 cup shredded unsweetened coconut
1 tablespoon ground flax
½ teaspoon salt
¾ cup coarsely chopped hazelnuts
½ cup dried blueberries

PER SERVING
(Serving size: 1 bar)

Calories: 148 · Fat: 9g

Protein: 2g · Sodium: 88mg

Fiber: 2g · Carbohydrates: 15g

Net Carbs: 13g · Sugar: 7g

1. Preheat oven to 350°F. Line a 9" × 9" pan with parchment paper.
2. In a medium bowl, combine bananas, oil, maple syrup, and vanilla extract and mix until well combined.
3. In a large bowl, combine oats, coconut, flax, salt, hazelnuts, and blueberries and mix well until combined.
4. Add the wet ingredients to the dry ingredients and mix well with a spatula until evenly incorporated.
5. Spread mixture out in an even layer in prepared pan. Bake 25–30 minutes or until lightly golden brown on top.
6. Let cool to room temperature. Once cool, cut into sixteen squares.

Pinto Bean Dip GF | DF | EF | NF | CT

This recipe is two in one. If you do it as written, it's a delicious bean dip that you can serve at events or as an after-school snack with vegetable sticks or home-made tortilla chips. Alternately, you can skip the blending step, and it becomes a yummy side dish to serve with tacos or with brown rice and greens. This version uses pinto beans, but black beans work really well too.

SERVES 8 | Prep Time: 10 minutes | Cook Time: 20 minutes

2 tablespoons extra-virgin olive oil

½ small red onion, peeled and diced small

2 cloves garlic, peeled and minced

1 tablespoon plus 1 teaspoon Tex-Mex Spice Blend (see Chapter 6)

1 (15-ounce) can crushed or diced tomatoes

½ cup water

¾ teaspoon salt

2 (15-ounce) cans pinto beans

½ cup chopped fresh cilantro

Juice from 2 medium limes

········ BABY FOOD ·······

This dip is a wonderful baby food recipe; just use less salt! Also for babies you'll want to blend the whole batch so there are no whole beans (the texture can still be a little chunky).

· · · · · · · · · · · · · · · · · · · ·

1. In a medium sauté pan over medium heat, heat oil. Add onions and sauté about 5 minutes.

2. Add garlic and Tex-Mex Spice Blend. Sauté 30 seconds, taking care not to let garlic burn.

3. Add tomatoes, water, and salt. Cook 7 minutes, smashing tomatoes with a wooden spoon.

4. In the meantime, drain and rinse beans under running water. Add beans to pan and smash them lightly with a wooden spoon. Cook another 7 minutes.

5. Remove pan from heat. Add cilantro and lime juice.

6. Remove 1 cup bean mixture and set aside. In a food processor, blend remaining bean mixture until it's mostly smooth but still a bit chunky. Add reserved beans to puréed beans and mix well. Serve.

PER SERVING

Calories: 128 · Fat: 4g · Protein: 6g · Sodium: 454mg

Fiber: 1g · Carbohydrates: 19g · Net Carbs: 18g · Sugar: 3g

Pico de Gallo GF | DF | EF | NF | CT

Pico de Gallo is a classic salsa that can be used in many different dishes or on its own for a great snack with homemade tortilla chips. It can be made ahead and kept refrigerated up to three days.

SERVES 4 | Prep Time: 10 minutes | Cook Time: n/a

2 large ripe tomatoes (about 1 pound), diced medium
¼ cup finely chopped onion
¼ cup small diced green bell pepper
¼ cup chopped fresh cilantro
2 tablespoons lime juice
¾ teaspoon salt
⅛ teaspoon cayenne pepper

1. In a medium bowl, combine all ingredients and mix well.
2. Taste and adjust seasonings if necessary.

PER SERVING

Calories: 23 · Fat: 0g
Protein: 1g · Sodium: 441mg
Fiber: 1g · Carbohydrates: 6g
Net Carbs: 5g · Sugar: 3g

· · · · · · · BABY FOOD · · · · · · ·

As is, this dish can be a choking hazard. Instead, purée the salsa (minus the salt) and use a spoonful as a seasoning for other foods, such as black beans, grains, or avocados.

Chickpea-Olive Smash GF | DF | EF | NF | CT

This dip is great with Homemade Pita Chips (see recipe in this chapter), on top of a salad, or in a pita with some roasted red peppers for a sophisticated plant-based lunch.

SERVES 8 | Prep Time: 20 minutes | Cook Time: n/a

1 (14-ounce) can chickpeas, drained and rinsed
¼ cup lemon juice
2 tablespoons chopped fresh parsley
3 tablespoons chopped pitted kalamata olives
½ teaspoon ground black pepper
½ teaspoon salt

1. In a medium bowl, using a fork or potato masher, mash chickpeas to the consistency of a chunky paste.
2. Add lemon juice, parsley, olives, pepper, and salt. Mix well and serve.

PER SERVING

Calories: 52 · Fat: 1g · Protein: 2g

Sodium: 256mg · Fiber: 2g

Carbohydrates: 8g · Net Carbs: 6g

Sugar: 1g

· · · · · · · **BABY FOOD** · · · · · · ·

This is a great recipe for babies. Eliminate the salt (olives are already salty) and make sure to mash well.

· ·

Guacamole GF | DF | EF | NF | CT

What better way to eat healthy plant-based fats than with delicious guacamole? This recipe is enhanced with an anti-inflammatory spice blend. If you want to turn down the heat, reduce the spices and eliminate the jalapeño. Serve as a snack with a platter of vegetable sticks like carrots, celery, and red peppers, or with homemade baked tortilla chips.

SERVES 6 | Prep Time: 15 minutes | Cook Time: n/a

3 medium ripe avocados

1 medium ripe tomato, finely diced

¼ cup finely diced red onion

¼ cup finely chopped cilantro

2 tablespoons fresh lime juice

½ teaspoon salt

1 teaspoon Tex-Mex Spice Blend (see Chapter 6)

1 medium jalapeño, seeds removed and minced

1. Cut avocados in half. Remove pit. Scoop out avocado flesh from the peel and put in a large bowl. Using a fork, mash avocados.

2. Add tomato, onion, cilantro, lime juice, salt, Tex-Mex Spice Blend, and jalapeño with avocados. Mix well to combine. Serve.

PER SERVING

Calories: 122 · Fat: 9g	
Protein: 2g · Sodium: 200mg	
Fiber: 5g · Carbohydrates: 8g	
Net Carbs: 3g · Sugar: 1g	

· · · · · · · BABY FOOD · · · · · · ·

For babies who are still learning to chew, eliminate the tomato and onion (or cut very finely). Also eliminate the spicy jalapeño.

· ·

Popcorn with Sweet Spiced Ghee GF | EF | NF | CT

Popcorn is a great conduit for any of the spice blends in this book. Here's one version, but the Savory Spiced Ghee or the Tex-Mex Spice Blend (both in Chapter 6) are also equally yummy. For a dairy-free version, use olive oil instead of ghee.

SERVES 4 | Prep Time: 5 minutes | Cook Time: 10 minutes

2 tablespoons avocado oil
½ cup popcorn kernels
2 tablespoons Sweet Spiced Ghee, melted (see Chapter 6)
¼ teaspoon salt

PER SERVING

Calories: 197 · Fat: 12g

Protein: 3g · Sodium: 146mg

Fiber: 3g · Carbohydrates: 22g

Net Carbs: 19g · Sugar: 5g

· · · · · · · BABY FOOD · · · · · · ·

Not recommended for babies and toddlers, as popcorn is a choking hazard.

1. In a large, heavy-bottomed pot, warm oil over medium heat.
2. Add two popcorn kernels to oil. Cover with a lid and wait until a pop is heard, about 2–4 minutes. Remove from heat.
3. Add remaining kernels and cover. Carefully shake pot with lid on to stir kernels.
4. Return to heat and shake pot frequently. All kernels should be popped after about 5 minutes.
5. Pour into a large bowl and top with Sweet Spiced Ghee and salt. Stir well to evenly coat popcorn.

Green Smoothie Bowl GF | DF | EF | NF | CT

This smoothie has a thick, slushy-like consistency and is fun served as a snack bowl. If you want to make it into a drinkable smoothie, simply increase the amount of water or add milk of choice.

SERVES 2 | Prep Time: 5 minutes | Cook Time: n/a

½ cup water
¼ cup frozen pineapple cubes
¼ cup tightly packed spinach
¼ cup ice
1 medium pitted date
1 medium banana, peeled and
    sliced in half, divided
1 tablespoon hemp seeds

1. In a blender, purée water, pineapple, spinach, ice, date, and half of banana until smooth and thick.
2. Divide into two bowls. Arrange remaining banana and hemp seeds on top. Serve.

PER SERVING
Calories: 125 · Fat: 2g · Protein: 3g
Sodium: 6mg · Fiber: 3g
Carbohydrates: 26g · Net Carbs: 23g
Sugar: 17g

· · · · · · · BABY FOOD · · · · · · ·

This is a fun recipe for babies! If they're not ready for slices of banana, purée the whole banana into the smoothie.

Pineapple-Papaya Skewers GF | DF | EF | NF | CT

If papaya isn't your thing, you can use mango or incorporate other fruits you like. For an even faster recipe, use precut fruit cubes, which are often available in the produce section.

SERVES 8 | Prep Time: 30 minutes | Cook Time: n/a

½ medium pineapple, peeled and diced large

1 medium papaya, peeled and diced large

16 skewers

¼ cup finely chopped fresh cilantro

2 medium limes, juiced

1 teaspoon Tex-Mex Spice Blend (see Chapter 6)

½ teaspoon salt

1. Place pineapple and papaya pieces on skewers (four to six pieces per skewer).
2. Sprinkle cilantro, lime juice, Tex-Mex Spice Blend, and salt over fruit and serve.

PER SERVING

(Serving size: 2 skewers)

Calories: 71 · Fat: 0g · Protein: 1g

Sodium: 153mg · Fiber: 3g

Carbohydrates: 18g · Net Carbs: 15g

Sugar: 13g

······ **BABY FOOD** ·······

For babies, simply purée the fruits with a bit of lime and cilantro.

Crispy Spiced Chickpeas   GF | DF | EF | NF | CT

Roasting chickpeas like this turns them into a crispy, addictive snack food...and one that's a lot healthier than potato chips! Change the flavor profile by experimenting with different spices, like the Tex-Mex or Sweet Spice blends in Chapter 6, or invent your own spice blend.

Phytonutrient focus: Chickpeas are rich in protein, fiber, calcium, magnesium, and many vitamins. They are also especially good sources of plant (or phyto-) sterols. Phytosterols are similar to human cholesterol. They therefore compete with cholesterol in the digestive system, blocking its absorption and lowering the overall rate of cholesterol in the body.

SERVES 4 | Prep Time: 10 minutes | Cook Time: 40 minutes

2 cups canned chickpeas, well rinsed and thoroughly drained
2 tablespoons avocado oil
½ teaspoon salt
1 tablespoon Basic Anti-Inflammatory Spice Blend (see Chapter 6)

······· BABY FOOD ·······

This dish is not recommended for babies due to the crispy texture. Instead, mash plain chickpeas with other cooked vegetables or purée with breastmilk or formula.

1. Preheat oven to 350°F. Line a baking sheet with parchment paper.
2. In a medium bowl, combine chickpeas with oil and salt.
3. Spread on baking sheet in a single layer and roast 20 minutes, stirring occasionally.
4. Increase heat to 400°F and continue roasting an additional 20 minutes.
5. While still hot from oven, return chickpeas to mixing bowl and toss with Basic Anti-Inflammatory Spice Blend. Serve immediately.

PER SERVING

Calories: 122 · Fat: 2g · Protein: 6g · Sodium: 453mg
Fiber: 6g · Carbohydrates: 19g · Net Carbs: 13g · Sugar: 3g

Sweet Potato Dumplings DF | EF | NF | CT

These dumplings are not a "quick and easy" after-school snack, but rather an activity for a weekend, rainy day, or small gathering.

SERVES 6 | Prep Time: 25 minutes | Cook Time: 1 hour

DIPPING SAUCE

¼ cup tamari

1 tablespoon brown rice vinegar

1 teaspoon honey

1 tablespoon water

1 tablespoon thinly sliced scallions

DUMPLINGS

2 small sweet potatoes

2 tablespoons plus 1½ teaspoons sesame oil, divided

1 (2") piece fresh ginger, peeled and minced

2 small leeks, white and light green parts only, cut finely into half-moons

¾ cup finely sliced shiitake mushrooms

3 cups finely sliced Napa cabbage

2 teaspoons tamari

2 teaspoons rice vinegar

¼ teaspoon salt

1 (12-ounce) package dumpling wrappers

PER SERVING

(Serving size: 4 dumplings)

Calories: 261 · Fat: 6g · Protein: 8g

Sodium: 1,195mg · Fiber: 3g

Carbohydrates: 43g · Net Carbs: 40g

Sugar: 5g

1. Preheat oven to 375°F. In a small bowl, combine all dipping sauce ingredients; set aside.

2. Bake potatoes 30–40 minutes until fork-tender.

3. Slice potatoes lengthwise, scoop out the flesh, and place in a medium bowl. Discard skin. Mash flesh with a fork until there are no lumps left.

4. While potatoes are baking, in a large sauté pan over medium heat, heat 1 tablespoon oil. Add ginger and leeks and sauté 3–5 minutes until leeks are translucent but not browned. Then add mushrooms, cabbage, tamari, vinegar, and salt. Sauté 10 minutes until cabbage is well wilted. Remove from heat.

5. Add leek mixture to the bowl with mashed sweet potatoes and mix well.

6. Fill a small bowl with warm water and set nearby.

7. Take a dumpling wrapper and place a spoonful of filling in middle. Using your fingertip, *lightly* wet outer rim of wrapper. Fold dumpling wrapper in half so it creates a half-moon shape and pinch edges together well. Repeat until all wrappers are used.

8. In a large sauté pan, heat 1½ teaspoons oil. Place dumplings in pan in a single layer.

9. When underside is browned and crispy, about 2 minutes, add 2 tablespoons water to pan and cover with a tight-fitting lid. Cook another 1–2 minutes and remove from heat. Repeat with rest of dumplings and oil.

10. Arrange dumplings on a platter with dipping sauce and serve.

CHAPTER 12

Desserts

Sweet treats can definitely be part of the anti-inflammatory way! Being healthy doesn't mean avoiding enjoyment. The desserts in this chapter are based on whole and naturally sweet ingredients, like fresh and dried fruits, whole grains, nuts, sweet vegetables like sweet potatoes, healthy fats, and of course delicious dark chocolate. A touch of honey and maple syrup add sweetness where necessary. On a daily basis, these treats—or a simple piece of fresh fruit in season—are your best choices.

And for those special occasions when a cake signals celebration, go for it! A healthy diet overall makes indulgences extra special and meaningful. The messages in the recipes can help guide your decisions. For example, our Coco-Cacao Energy Bites are a good everyday sweet treat, while the Torta di Mandorle is a special-occasion dessert.

Please note that most of these recipes do not have modifications for babies. For little ones under two years old, a variety of mashed fruits are plenty sweet and the only desserts they need.

Spiced Chocolate Fondue with Fruit Kebabs GF | EF | NF | CT

This recipe turns simple fresh fruit and dark chocolate into a special occasion. Kids love making the fruit kebabs. It's a great activity for even a large group at a birthday party or other gathering. Kebab skewers have a pointy end, so for young children (five years old and under) use Popsicle sticks, which have rounded ends. Feel free to use other fruits such as pineapple, cantaloupe, or grapes. Substitute a milk alternative if you wish to make it dairy-free. If there are leftovers, the fondue can be held in the refrigerator for up to one week and rewarmed.

SERVES 4 | Prep Time: 20 minutes | Cook Time: 5 minutes

*2 medium bananas, cut into 2"
    slices*
*2 medium kiwi, peeled, halved,
    and cut into 2" half-moons*
*8 medium strawberries, tops
    removed and cut in half
    lengthwise*
8 kebab skewers
*¼ cup plus 2 tablespoons whole
    milk*
*1¼ cups dark chocolate chips
    (60% cacao or higher)*
1 teaspoon vanilla extract
*1 teaspoon Sweet Spice Blend (see
    Chapter 6)*

1. Make fruit kebabs by skewering bananas, kiwi, and strawberries onto kebabs, alternating colors. Set aside.

2. In a small saucepot over medium-high heat, heat milk until just boiling.

3. Reduce heat to low. Add chocolate, vanilla, and Sweet Spice Blend to milk. Stir until melted and well combined.

4. Place melted chocolate in a serving bowl or small individual bowls if for a group of kids. Dip fruit in and enjoy!

PER SERVING

Calories: 391 · Fat: 17g	
Protein: 5g · Sodium: 23mg	
Fiber: 7g · Carbohydrates: 54g	
Net Carbs: 47g · Sugar: 37g	

Dark Chocolate Bark GF | DF | EF | CT

Dark chocolate is packed with flavonoids and is an excellent dessert in moderation. This bark is a very customizable recipe. The base recipe combines 1 cup total of toppings, such as dried fruit, nuts, or seeds, plus 1 teaspoon total spices, such as cinnamon, chili peppers, ginger, sea salt, or citrus zest. We suggest a few different flavor combinations, but follow your creativity!

SERVES 8 | Prep Time: 10 minutes, 2 hours passive | Cook Time: 5 minutes

2 cups dark chocolate chips
    (60% cacao or higher)
½ cup chopped dried figs
½ cup chopped pecans
½ teaspoon orange zest
½ teaspoon fennel seeds, roughly
    crushed or chopped

FLAVOR COMBINATIONS

Try these combinations:

• Sweet Spice Blend (see Chapter 6), dried coconut, dried mango, and cashews
• Dried cherries, hazelnuts, cacao nibs, and sea salt
• Pumpkin seeds, dried papaya, chili powder, and cinnamon
• Dried apricots, sesame seeds, turmeric, and cardamom
• Za'atar, almonds, and dates

1. Line a cookie sheet with parchment paper.
2. Fill a medium saucepan ⅓ of the way with water. Place a medium bowl on top. It should fit securely, but bottom of bowl should not touch bottom of pot. Place chocolate chips in bowl and melt, stirring occasionally. (Alternately, melt chocolate in the microwave.)
3. Once chocolate is smooth and melted, pour it onto cookie sheet. Spread with a spatula into a thin, even layer.
4. Sprinkle evenly with figs, pecans, orange zest, and fennel seeds, and place in refrigerator to set at least 2 hours or overnight.
5. Once set, break into pieces and serve.

PER SERVING

Calories: 304 · Fat: 17g · Protein: 3g · Sodium: 10mg			
Fiber: 5g · Carbohydrates: 32g · Net Carbs: 27g · Sugar: 24g			

Chai Chia Pudding GF | DF | EF | NF | CT

This is a no-cook pudding that makes an easy dessert or breakfast. If you don't love the texture of chia seeds, combine all the ingredients in a blender, blend for a minute, and then let it sit in the refrigerator. It will still thicken into pudding, but will have a smoother consistency. This pudding can be eaten as is or topped with fruit, nuts, granola, dark chocolate, or jam.

Phytonutrient focus: When combined with liquid, chia seeds swell and become gooey, which is a product of their polysaccharides (i.e., fiber). These are beneficial to our digestive systems and help control blood sugar. Chia is also very high in omega-3 fats and a good source of protein, iron, calcium, and many anti-inflammatory phytochemicals.

SERVES 2 | Prep Time: 5 minutes, 2 hours passive | Cook Time: n/a

½ cup plus 2 tablespoons canned unsweetened coconut milk
½ teaspoon Sweet Spice Blend (see Chapter 6)
1 teaspoon pure maple syrup
2 tablespoons chia seeds

1. In a small pot, over low heat, warm milk just until it achieves a liquid and uniform consistency.

2. In a medium bowl or Mason jar, combine milk, Sweet Spice Blend, maple syrup, and chia seeds. Stir well to combine or, if in a jar, shake well. Place in refrigerator with a tight-fitting lid for at least 2 hours.

3. Remove from refrigerator and eat as is.

PER SERVING

Calories: 232 · Fat: 20g

Protein: 3g · Sodium: 12mg

Fiber: 5g · Carbohydrates: 11g

Net Carbs: 6g · Sugar: 5g

· · · · · · BABY FOOD · · · · · · ·

This recipe is good for babies, minus the maple syrup and toppings.

· ·

Jam Dots GF | DF | EF | CT

These gluten-free cookies are high in protein, fiber, and healthy fats because of the almond flour. And they're super fun to make! If you don't have homemade jam, substitute with a high-quality store-bought jam. You may also use melted butter in place of coconut oil if you wish.

YIELDS 12 COOKIES | Prep Time: 10 minutes | Cook Time: 15 minutes

¼ cup melted coconut oil

3 tablespoons pure maple syrup

½ teaspoon vanilla extract

2 cups almond flour

1 teaspoon ground cinnamon

⅛ teaspoon salt

⅓ cup Berry Ginger Jam (see Chapter 6)

PER SERVING

(Serving size: 1 cookie)

Calories: 163 · Fat: 14g

Protein: 4g · Sodium: 24mg

Fiber: 2g · Carbohydrates: 8g

Net Carbs: 6g · Sugar: 4g

1. Preheat oven to 325°F. Line a baking sheet with parchment paper.
2. In a large bowl, combine oil, maple syrup, and vanilla. Add flour, cinnamon, and salt. Stir into a thick batter.
3. Roll cookies into ¾" balls. Place on baking sheet 1"–1½" apart. Flatten slightly into a disk shape. Using thumb, press an indentation into middle of each cookie. Place about 1 teaspoon jam into each indentation.
4. Bake 12–15 minutes until cookies are golden brown. Remove from oven and cool. Cookies will firm up once completely cool.

Mango-Peach Frozen Yogurt GF | EF | NF | CT

Did you know you could make your own frozen yogurt? It's incredibly simple! It's great eaten on its own, and for special occasions, you can turn it into a banana split or a sundae with toppings like nuts, dark chocolate chips, or fruit. Another great idea is to substitute the peach and mango with frozen mixed berries.

SERVES 6 | Prep Time: 15 minutes, plus 4 hours to overnight, passive | Cook Time: n/a

2½ cups whole milk vanilla yogurt
1½ cups frozen peaches
1 cup frozen mango chunks
½ medium orange, zested

PER SERVING

Calories: 138 · Fat: 3g	
Protein: 4g · Sodium: 50mg	
Fiber: 2g · Carbohydrates: 24g	
Net Carbs: 22g · Sugar: 22g	

· · · · · · · BABY FOOD · · · · · · ·

This recipe can be good for babies if you substitute plain yogurt.

1. Line an 8" × 8" baking pan with parchment paper. Spread yogurt onto pan. Place yogurt in freezer at least 4 hours or overnight.
2. Remove from freezer and break into big chunks with a fork.
3. In a food processor, combine yogurt, peaches, mango, and orange zest. Pulse until a thick purée is made with fruit evenly distributed. Serve.

White Tea and Strawberry Granita GF | DF | EF | NF | CT

This is a great early-summer treat when strawberries are at their peak, or you can also use frozen berries if that's all you can find. You may also substitute other fruits such as peaches, plums, apricots, and melons. It is high in antioxidants from the fruit and tea. Get kids involved by having them scrape the ice with a fork as it freezes.

SERVES 8 | Prep Time: 20 minutes, 2–3 hours passive | Cook Time: n/a

4 cups hot water
2 medium pitted dates
2 white tea bags (decaffeinated if children under twelve years old are served)
2 cups strawberries

PER SERVING

Calories: 17 · Fat: 0g	
Protein: 0g · Sodium: 3mg	
Fiber: 1g · Carbohydrates: 4g	
Net Carbs: 3g · Sugar: 3g	

1. Place hot water in a large bowl or pitcher. Add dates and tea bags. Steep 20 minutes.
2. Remove tea bags. Cool.
3. Pour cooled tea and dates into blender. Add strawberries. Blend until smooth.
4. Pour blended mixture into a large glass casserole dish and place in freezer for 2 hours. (If frozen for much longer than that, it becomes harder to scrape.)
5. Remove from freezer and scrape thoroughly with a fork into small ice crystals. If bottom layers are not yet frozen enough to scrape, return to freezer for another hour and repeat scraping.
6. Serve in parfait cups.

Coco-Cacao Energy Bites GF | DF | EF | CT | NF

Sweetened with dates and full of plant-based nutrients, these are an everyday dessert or snack you can feel very good about serving.

SERVES 24 | Prep Time: 20 minutes, plus 30 minutes to overnight refrigeration | Cook Time: n/a

½ cup sunflower seeds
¼ cup pumpkin seeds
20 medium whole dates, pitted
    and roughly chopped
¾ cup shredded unsweetened
    coconut, divided
½ cup unsweetened cacao powder,
    divided
2 tablespoons coconut oil
⅛ teaspoon salt
1½ tablespoons water

PER SERVING

(Serving size: 1 ball)

Calories: 72 · Fat: 5g

Protein: 2g · Sodium: 12mg

Fiber: 2g · Carbohydrates: 7g

Net Carbs: 5g · Sugar: 4g

1. Put seeds in a food processor and pulse until they are finely chopped (but not super fine like a powder).

2. Add dates, ½ cup shredded coconut, ¼ cup cacao, oil, salt, and water and process until ingredients are well mixed and mixture looks uniform.

3. Using a tablespoon, spoon out mixture and roll into balls.

4. Put remaining ¼ cup shredded coconut and ¼ cup cacao on two separate flat plates. Coat balls with cacao or coconut by rolling half of balls in one, and half in the other. Place completed balls on a parchment paper–lined baking sheet.

5. Refrigerate at least 30 minutes (or up to overnight) until they harden. They will keep in refrigerator in an airtight container or plastic bag up to two weeks.

Chocolate Silken Tofu Pudding GF | DF | EF | NF | CT

This is a rich and silky pudding. Top with a generous portion of fresh fruit to give it brightness, both in color and flavor.

SERVES 8 | Prep Time: 15 minutes, 1 hour passive | Cook Time: n/a

2 cups dark chocolate chips (60% cacao or higher)
1 pound silken tofu
1 teaspoon vanilla extract

PER SERVING

Calories: 270 · Fat: 14g

Protein: 6g · Sodium: 30mg

Fiber: 3g · Carbohydrates: 27g

Net Carbs: 24g · Sugar: 20g

1. Fill a medium saucepan ⅓ of the way with water. Place a medium bowl on top. It should fit securely, but bottom of bowl should not touch bottom of pot. Place chocolate in bowl and melt, stirring occasionally. (A double boiler may be used or you can melt chocolate in the microwave.)

2. In a blender, combine tofu, melted chocolate, and vanilla. Blend until smooth.

3. Pour into a glass container, cover, and refrigerate at least 1 hour. Serve.

Frozen Banana Pops GF | EF | CT

This recipe takes an everyday fruit and transforms it into a special treat. Kids can participate in the whole process and especially enjoy drizzling the chocolate to make elaborate decorations. Substitute a dairy-free yogurt if you wish.

SERVES 4 | Prep Time: 15 minutes, plus 2 hours freeze time | Cook Time: n/a

¼ cup dark chocolate chips (60% cacao or higher)
2 large ripe bananas
4 Popsicle sticks
½ cup plain, whole milk Greek yogurt
½ cup Anti-Inflammatory Granola, crushed into small chunks (see Chapter 7)

PER SERVING
Calories: 235 · Fat: 11g
Protein: 6g · Sodium: 31mg
Fiber: 4g · Carbohydrates: 29g
Net Carbs: 25g · Sugar: 17g

1. Prepare a baking sheet with parchment paper. Be sure tray will fit in a freezer.

2. Fill a medium saucepan ⅓ of the way with water. Place a medium bowl on top of it. It should fit securely, but bottom of bowl should not touch bottom of pot. Place chocolate in bowl and melt, stirring occasionally. (A double boiler may also be used or you can melt chocolate in the microwave.)

3. Peel bananas and cut them in half crosswise. Insert sticks into cut ends of bananas.

4. Place yogurt in a small shallow bowl.

5. Place granola on a flat plate.

6. To assemble, dip and roll banana in yogurt. Spread with back of a spoon or pastry brush to make sure it is well coated. Then roll banana in granola until it is evenly coated. Use your fingers to gently help granola stick.

7. Place banana pops on sheet and drizzle melted chocolate evenly over them. It's okay if the excess goes onto parchment paper.

8. Place tray in freezer at least 2 hours or up to overnight to firm up toppings. Serve.

Sweet Potato Cookies EF | NF | CT

These cookies are inspired by *mbatata*, a traditional cake-like cookie from Malawi, where sweet potatoes are a staple food. Try gluten-free flour and/or coconut oil and a milk alternative to accommodate allergies.

Phytonutrient focus: Cinnamon is an old medicine in many parts of the world, often associated with blood health. Indeed, research has shown that it promotes healthy blood circulation, lower lipid levels, and healthy blood sugar levels. In other words, it can help protect against cardiovascular disease and diabetes. It is especially wonderful added to sweet foods like these cookies, where it can play its part to regulate blood sugar, insulin, and inflammation.

YIELDS 24 COOKIES | Prep Time: 20 minutes | Cook Time: 20 minutes

1 cup mashed cooked sweet potatoes
4 tablespoons unsalted butter, melted
2 tablespoons whole milk
⅓ cup honey
1 tablespoon plus 1 teaspoon baking powder
½ teaspoon salt
2 teaspoons ground cinnamon
2 cups whole-wheat pastry flour
¼ cup plus 2 tablespoons raisins

PER SERVING

(Serving size: 1 cookie)	
Calories: 80 · Fat: 2g	
Protein: 1g · Sodium: 133mg	
Fiber: 2g · Carbohydrates: 16g	
Net Carbs: 14g · Sugar: 6g	

1. Preheat oven to 350°F.

2. In a large bowl, combine mashed sweet potatoes and butter.

3. Add milk, honey, baking powder, salt, and cinnamon and mix to combine.

4. Fold in flour until it is evenly incorporated. Then fold in raisins until they are evenly distributed. The batter will be thick and sticky.

5. Working with clean, lightly wet hands, pinch off a piece of the batter and roll into about a 1" ball between your palms. Then lightly press it into a disk shape and put on a baking sheet. Repeat with remaining batter, yielding twenty-four cookies. If dough begins to stick to your hands, clean them and start again, always with lightly wet hands.

6. Bake cookies about 17 minutes. They will be firm but still pale on top. Remove from oven and let cool 10 minutes before serving.

Peach-Raspberry Crumble DF | EF | CT

Crumbles are a great choice for anti-inflammatory desserts because they are mostly fruit with the topping as an extra treat. This is a version that is best at the height of late summer, when peaches and raspberries are abundant. In fall, substitute apples or pears instead of peaches. And any time of year, you can use frozen fruit. Use gluten-free flour or leave out the nuts to accommodate allergies.

SERVES 10 | Prep Time: 20 minutes | Cook Time: 40 minutes

5 medium fresh peaches, peeled and cut into ¼" slices

1 pint fresh raspberries

½ cup pure maple syrup, divided

¾ cup plus 1 tablespoon whole-wheat pastry flour, divided

½ cup rolled oats (not instant)

½ cup roughly chopped pecans

¼ teaspoon salt

5 tablespoons extra-virgin olive oil

PER SERVING

Calories: 230 · Fat: 11g	
Protein: 3g · Sodium: 60mg	
Fiber: 5g · Carbohydrates: 32g	
Net Carbs: 27g · Sugar: 17g	

1. Preheat oven to 350°F.

2. In a large bowl, combine peaches, raspberries, ¼ cup maple syrup, and 1 tablespoon flour and mix well. Pour fruit mixture into a 9" round baking pan and set aside.

3. In a medium bowl, combine remaining ¾ cup flour, oats, pecans, and salt and mix well. Add remaining ¼ cup maple syrup and oil. Gently mix until flour and oats are evenly moist. Toward end of mixing, your fingers can be used to press mixture into different-sized crumbles—some will be fine and other parts will be larger clumps.

4. Pour crumble topping loosely over fruit, covering evenly.

5. Bake 40 minutes until crumble top is golden brown and fruit has bubbled up.

6. Remove from oven and let cool at least 30 minutes before serving.

Torta di Mandorle (Almond–Orange Torte) GF | DF | CT

This is based on a traditional Italian almond torte that is naturally gluten-free and dairy-free and still quite rich. Note that it calls for nut "meals" instead of nut flours. Meals are a bit more coarsely ground than flour and contribute to a lovely texture. That said, you may use flour as long as it's not super finely ground.

Phytonutrient focus: Like all nuts, sweet almonds are full of protein, fiber, and fats that are protective to brain and heart health. They have strong antioxidant properties, which means they help to reduce inflammation and protect against cancer. Almond flour is especially great in gluten-free baking, as in this recipe.

SERVES 16 | Prep Time: 45 minutes | Cook Time: 1 hour 30 minutes

3 large oranges

2 bay leaves

1 cinnamon stick

¾ cup Sucanat (or sugar)

6 large eggs

½ teaspoon baking powder

3½ cups almond meal

1 cup hazelnut meal

¾ cup dark chocolate chips (60% cacao or higher)

PER SERVING

Calories: 296 · Fat: 19g

Protein: 9g · Sodium: 43mg

Fiber: 5g · Carbohydrates: 24g

Net Carbs: 19g · Sugar: 15g

1. Preheat oven to 350°F. Grease and flour a 9" × 13" pan.
2. In a medium pot, combine oranges, bay leaves, and cinnamon and cover with water. Bring to a boil and simmer over low heat 45 minutes until oranges are easily pierced with a fork. Cut them in quarters and let cool. Take out seeds and blend in a food processor (yes, skin and all) until mash is chunky but even.
3. In a large bowl, combine orange purée, Sucanat, eggs, baking powder, and nut meals. Mix well, then fold in chocolate chips.
4. Pour batter into prepared cake pan. Bake 40–45 minutes.
5. Let cool at least 30 minutes before serving.

Apple Cake NF | CT

This cake is made up of mostly apples, with a little batter to hold it together. The first time you make it, you may feel as if there's not quite enough batter to cover the apples, but it's a tried-and-true recipe, so trust it! It will quickly become a family favorite. In place of whole-wheat pastry flour, regular whole-wheat flour or gluten-free flour works. And if you wish, use coconut oil instead of butter.

SERVES 10 | Prep Time: 20 minutes | Cook Time: 30 minutes

3 large Granny Smith apples, peeled
1 cup whole-wheat pastry flour
1 teaspoon baking powder
3 large eggs
½ cup Sucanat (or sugar)
¾ stick (6 tablespoons) butter, melted and cooled to room temperature
1 teaspoon vanilla extract
¼ teaspoon salt
½ medium lemon, zested

PER SERVING

Calories: 198 · Fat: 8g
Protein: 3g · Sodium: 129mg
Fiber: 3g · Carbohydrates: 28g
Net Carbs: 25g · Sugar: 15g

1. Preheat oven to 350°F. Butter and flour either a 9" × 9" square or 9" round cake pan.

2. Quarter apples, remove core, and slice very thin. Place apple slices in a large bowl with cold water to keep them from turning brown.

3. In a large bowl, combine flour and baking powder. Mix well and set aside.

4. In a medium bowl, combine eggs, Sucanat, butter, vanilla, salt, and lemon zest. Mix well.

5. Pour wet mixture into dry and mix with spatula until just combined. Do not overmix.

6. Reserve about ten apple slices for decorating the top. Gently fold remaining apples into batter and pour mixture into baking pan.

7. Smooth top of cake with a spatula and arrange reserved apples in desired pattern on top.

8. Bake on center rack 25–30 minutes or until toothpick inserted into center comes out clean and cake is nicely browned on top. Serve.

CHAPTER 13

Beverages

The default beverage for the anti-inflammatory table should always be water—start there. Put plain or sparkling water on the table for every meal. If you wish, add slices of fruits such as strawberries, oranges, and limes, and/or herbs such as basil and mint.

But sometimes you may want something a little more festive and interesting than water. In the US, beverages tend to have a negative impact on health—sodas, energy drinks, sweetened teas and coffees, and even juice. This chapter will offer you some fun alternatives. If juice or soda are staples of your meals, try the Juice Spritzer instead.

Beverages can also be wonderful vehicles for anti-inflammatory nutrients—smoothies deliver whole fruits and vegetables, and the chai and herbal teas are wonderful sources of anti-inflammatory phytochemicals.

The recipes in this chapter are just the tip of the iceberg. Use them as templates and experiment! Note that most of these beverages, including those that include tea or juice, are not appropriate for babies under two years old.

Chocolate-Blueberry Smoothie GF | EF | NF | CT

This smoothie is nutrient-dense and delicious, especially for picky eaters or teens on the run. Use a milk alternative to make it dairy-free.

SERVES 2 | Prep Time: 5 minutes | Cook Time: n/a

½ cup whole milk

½ cup frozen blueberries

¼ cup cold silken tofu

1 tablespoon unsweetened cacao powder

½ teaspoon ground cinnamon

1 medium pitted date

In a blender or food processor, purée all ingredients until smooth. Serve.

PER SERVING

Calories: 98 · Fat: 3g

Protein: 5g · Sodium: 37mg

Fiber: 2g · Carbohydrates: 13g

Net Carbs: 11g · Sugar: 9g

· · · · · · BABY FOOD · · · · · · ·

Mix a bit of this smoothie in with oatmeal or other grains, minus the cacao powder, which has caffeine. Do not give to babies in a baby bottle.

Golden Milk Smoothie GF | DF | EF | NF | CT

This smoothie is a super tasty boost of anti-inflammatory phytochemicals. Using whole milk in place of the coconut milk is also delicious.

SERVES 1 | Prep Time: 5 minutes | Cook Time: n/a

½ cup canned unsweetened coconut milk
½ cup mashed ripe banana
1 medium pitted date
½ teaspoon ground turmeric
1 teaspoon Sweet Spice Blend (see
Chapter 6)
Pinch (less than ⅛ teaspoon)
ground black pepper

In a blender or food processor, purée all ingredients until smooth. If you like it very cold, add a couple of ice cubes to the blender or serve over ice.

PER SERVING

Calories: 81 · Fat: 5g

Protein: 1g · Sodium: 3mg

Fiber: 1g · Carbohydrates: 8g

Net Carbs: 7g · Sugar: 4g

· · · · · · BABY FOOD · · · · · · ·

Mix a bit of this smoothie in with oatmeal or other grains. Do not give to babies in a baby bottle.

Immune-Boosting Hot Cocoa GF | EF | NF

The medicinal qualities of this delicious cocoa come from two powerful herbs, licorice and astragalus. In the winter, serve this a few times per week as an after-dinner treat to help boost the function of your family's immune systems. You can find astragalus in powder form online or in some natural foods stores. Feel free to substitute any milk you wish.

SERVES 1 | Prep Time: 3 minutes | Cook Time: 5 minutes

½ cup whole milk
½ cup water
1 licorice root tea bag (or 1 teaspoon licorice root)
1 tablespoon unsweetened cocoa powder
¼ teaspoon Sweet Spice Blend (see Chapter 6)
¼ teaspoon turmeric
1 teaspoon astragalus powder
1 teaspoon pure maple syrup

In a small pot over low heat, add all the ingredients and simmer 5 minutes. Whisk well to make sure ingredients are well combined. Serve hot.

PER SERVING

Calories: 118 · Fat: 4g

Protein: 5g · Sodium: 84mg

Fiber: 2g · Carbohydrates: 16g

Net Carbs: 14g · Sugar: 10g

······· BABY FOOD ·······

This recipe is not appropriate for babies.

Strawberry "Milk" GF | EF | NF | CT

This is a nutritious alternative to sweetened milk drinks like strawberry or chocolate milk. It is delicious with other frozen fruit as well, like sweet cherries, mangoes, or blueberries.

Phytonutrient focus: Strawberries are not technically botanical berries. But they are supercharged with antioxidant qualities that help protect our cells, DNA, and overall health. They are also one of nature's finest desserts—dipped in chocolate, blended into this smoothie, or all by themselves. Strawberries are one of the most heavily sprayed fruits, so when you can, choose organic.

SERVES 2 | Prep Time: 5 minutes | Cook Time: n/a

⅓ cup hot water
1 decaffeinated white tea bag
1 ice cube
½ cup frozen strawberries
½ cup plain, whole milk yogurt
1 medium pitted date
½ teaspoon ground cinnamon

1. In a mug, pour water over tea bag and let steep 3 minutes. Remove tea bag and add ice cube to cool it down.
2. In a blender or food processor, combine tea with all other ingredients and purée until smooth.

PER SERVING

Calories: 61 · Fat: 2g
Protein: 2g · Sodium: 29mg
Fiber: 1g · Carbohydrates: 10g
Net Carbs: 9g · Sugar: 7g

······· BABY FOOD ·······

Mix a bit of this smoothie in with oatmeal or other grains, minus the white tea. Do not give to babies in a baby bottle.

······························

Juice Spritzer GF | DF | EF | NF | CT

Although 100 percent juice doesn't have any added sugar, it still acts like sugar in the body. This recipe reduces the sugar and adds the sparkle of seltzer. You may do the same with plain water if you don't want the bubble. And remember that plain water or seltzer should still be your family's everyday beverage.

SERVES 1 | Prep Time: 2 minutes | Cook Time: n/a

¼ cup 100 percent fruit juice
¾ cup seltzer or sparkling water
Ice cubes, if desired
1 lemon wedge

1. In a glass, combine juice and seltzer or sparkling water. Add ice if desired.
2. Garnish with lemon wedge and serve. If making a pitcherful, simply fill it up ¼ juice and ¾ seltzer or sparkling water.

PER SERVING

Calories: 32 · Fat: 0g

Protein: 0g · Sodium: 26mg

Fiber: 0g · Carbohydrates: 7g

Net Carbs: 7g · Sugar: 6g

· · · · · · · BABY FOOD · · · · · · ·

This drink is not appropriate for babies under two years old because of the juice.

Green Tea Chai GF | EF | NF

Green tea plus spices equals a delicious daily dose of anti-inflammatory compounds. Here, the grassy taste of green tea is transformed into a creamy, aromatic beverage. This recipe is for teens and adults, especially those wanting to wean themselves off expensive, sugary coffees and teas. If you want to get real fancy, froth the milk! (Coconut milk is a delicious, dairy-free alternative.) And if you wish, add a teaspoon of honey to sweeten.

SERVES 1 | Prep Time: 3 minutes | Cook Time: n/a

2 tablespoons whole milk
1 teaspoon Sweet Spice Blend (see
    Chapter 6)
1 bag green tea
1 cup boiling hot water

1. In a cup, combine milk, Sweet Spice Blend, and tea bag.
2. Pour water over and let steep 3 minutes or according to tea package instructions. Stir well and serve hot.

PER SERVING

Calories: 26 · Fat: 1g

Protein: 1g · Sodium: 12mg

Fiber: 1g · Carbohydrates: 4g

Net Carbs: 3g · Sugar: 2g

······ BABY FOOD ·······

This drink is not appropriate
for babies.

Chilled Rooibos Tea GF | DF | EF | NF

Rooibos is a traditional South African herbal tea. It is especially rich in phyto-nutrients, and, like all herbal teas, it has no caffeine. In this recipe, it is lightly sweetened with orange juice. Serve instead of soda or juice at your next meal.

SERVES 4 | Prep Time: 10 minutes, plus time for chilling | Cook Time: n/a

4 cups water

4 teaspoons loose rooibos tea (or 4 rooibos tea bags)

1 teaspoon Sweet Spice Blend (see Chapter 6)

1 teaspoon vanilla extract

Ice cubes, if desired

1 cup orange juice

1 medium orange, cut into thin slices

1. In a medium saucepan over high heat, heat water to boiling and then turn off heat. Add tea and let steep 10 minutes. Strain and discard tea (or tea bags).

2. Stir in Sweet Spice Blend and vanilla. Let cool to room temperature and then chill, either by adding ice cubes or putting in the refrigerator.

3. Once chilled, stir in orange juice. Serve cold, garnished with orange slices.

PER SERVING

Calories: 34 · Fat: 0g

Protein: 0g · Sodium: 2mg

Fiber: 0g · Carbohydrates: 7g

Net Carbs: 7g · Sugar: 5g

· · · · · · · BABY FOOD · · · · · · ·

This drink is not appropriate for babies.

· ·

Soothing Summer Tea GF | DF | EF | NF

Mint and lemon balm make a delicious, refreshing summer tea. These herbs can also be gentle remedies for bellyaches, and lemon balm is especially calming for kids in cases of mild anxiety or hyperactivity. Here, we sweeten the tea lightly with tart cherry juice, which is among the most antioxidant-rich fruits. Pomegranate juice would also be a nice choice.

SERVES 4 | Prep Time: 8 minutes, plus time for chilling | Cook Time: n/a

4 cups water

2 tablespoons tightly packed chopped fresh mint leaves

4 bags lemon balm tea (or 4 teaspoons dried lemon balm leaves)

Ice cubes, if desired

1 cup 100% tart cherry juice

3 sprigs fresh mint

1. In a small saucepan over high heat, heat water to boiling, then turn off heat. Add mint and lemon balm, cover with a lid, and let steep 8 minutes.

2. Let cool to room temperature and then chill, either by adding ice cubes or putting in the refrigerator.

3. Once chilled, stir in cherry juice and serve, garnished with fresh mint sprigs.

PER SERVING

Calories: 40 · Fat: 0g

Protein: 1g · Sodium: 65mg

Fiber: 0g · Carbohydrates: 9g

Net Carbs: 9g · Sugar: 6g

· · · · · · · BABY FOOD · · · · · · ·

This drink is not appropriate for babies under two years old because of the juice.

· ·

Standard US/Metric Measurement Conversions

VOLUME CONVERSIONS

US Volume Measure	Metric Equivalent
⅛ teaspoon	0.5 milliliter
¼ teaspoon	1 milliliter
½ teaspoon	2 milliliters
1 teaspoon	5 milliliters
½ tablespoon	7 milliliters
1 tablespoon (3 teaspoons)	15 milliliters
2 tablespoons (1 fluid ounce)	30 milliliters
¼ cup (4 tablespoons)	60 milliliters
⅓ cup	90 milliliters
½ cup (4 fluid ounces)	125 milliliters
⅔ cup	160 milliliters
¾ cup (6 fluid ounces)	180 milliliters
1 cup (16 tablespoons)	250 milliliters
1 pint (2 cups)	500 milliliters
1 quart (4 cups)	1 liter (about)

WEIGHT CONVERSIONS

US Weight Measure	Metric Equivalent
½ ounce	15 grams
1 ounce	30 grams
2 ounces	60 grams
3 ounces	85 grams
¼ pound (4 ounces)	115 grams
½ pound (8 ounces)	225 grams
¾ pound (12 ounces)	340 grams
1 pound (16 ounces)	454 grams

OVEN TEMPERATURE CONVERSIONS

Degrees Fahrenheit	Degrees Celsius
200 degrees F	95 degrees C
250 degrees F	120 degrees C
275 degrees F	135 degrees C
300 degrees F	150 degrees C
325 degrees F	160 degrees C
350 degrees F	180 degrees C
375 degrees F	190 degrees C
400 degrees F	205 degrees C
425 degrees F	220 degrees C
450 degrees F	230 degrees C

BAKING PAN SIZES

American	Metric
8 × 1½ inch round baking pan	20 × 4 cm cake tin
9 × 1½ inch round baking pan	23 × 3.5 cm cake tin
11 × 7 × 1½ inch baking pan	28 × 18 × 4 cm baking tin
13 × 9 × 2 inch baking pan	30 × 20 × 5 cm baking tin
2 quart rectangular baking dish	30 × 20 × 3 cm baking tin
15 × 10 × 2 inch baking pan	30 × 25 × 2 cm baking tin (Swiss roll tin)
9 inch pie plate	22 × 4 or 23 × 4 cm pie plate
7 or 8 inch springform pan	18 or 20 cm springform or loose bottom cake tin
9 × 5 × 3 inch loaf pan	23 × 13 × 7 cm or 2 lb narrow loaf or pate tin
1½ quart casserole	1.5 liter casserole
2 quart casserole	2 liter casserole

References

CHAPTER 1

What Is the Anti-Inflammatory Way?

Serra-Majem, Lluis, Blanca Román-Viñas, Almudena Sanchez-Villegas, Marta Guasch-Ferré, Dolores Corella, and Carlo La Vecchia. "Benefits of the Mediterranean Diet: Epidemiological and Molecular Aspects." *Molecular Aspects of Medicine* 67 (June 2019): 1–55. https://doi.org/10.1016/j.mam.2019.06.001.

Abenavoli, Ludovico, Luigi Boccuto, Alessandro Federico, Marcello Dallio, Carmelina Loguercio, Laura Di Renzo, and Antonino De Lorenzo. "Diet and Non-Alcoholic Fatty Liver Disease: The Mediterranean Way." *International Journal of Environmental Research and Public Health* 16, no. 17 (August 21, 2019): 3,011. https://doi.org/10.3390/ijerph16173011.

Hernáez, Álvaro, and Ramón Estruch. "The Mediterranean Diet and Cancer: What Do Human and Molecular Studies Have to Say about It?" *Nutrients* 11, no. 9 (September 9, 2019): 2,155. https://doi.org/10.3390/nu11092155.

Khalili, Hamed, Niclas Håkansson, Simon S. Chan, Ye Chen, Paul Lochhead, Jonas F. Ludvigsson, Andrew T. Chan, Andrew R. Hart, Ola Olén, and Alicja Wolk. "Adherence to a Mediterranean Diet Is Associated with a Lower Risk of Later-Onset Crohn's Disease: Results from Two Large Prospective Cohort Studies." *Gut* (January 3, 2020): gutjnl-2019-319505. https://doi.org/10.1136/gutjnl-2019-319505.

Mascarenhas, Maria R. "Pediatric Anti-Inflammatory Diet." *Pediatric Annals* 48, no. 6 (June 1, 2019): e220–25. https://doi.org/10.3928/19382359-20190515-02.

Agakidis, Charalampos, Evangelia Kotzakioulafi, Dimitrios Petridis, Konstantina Apostolidou, and Thomai Karagiozoglou-Lampoudi. "Mediterranean Diet Adherence Is Associated with Lower Prevalence of Functional Gastrointestinal Disorders in Children and Adolescents." *Nutrients* 11, no. 6 (June 6, 2019): 1,283. https://doi.org/10.3390/nu11061283.

Navarrete-Muñoz, Eva-María, Paula Fernández-Pires, Silvia Navarro-Amat, Miriam Hurtado-Pomares, Paula Peral-Gómez, Iris Juárez-Leal, Cristina Espinosa-Sempere, Alicia Sánchez-Pérez, and Desirée Valera-Gran. "Association between Adherence to the Antioxidant-Rich Mediterranean Diet and Sensory Processing Profile in School-Aged Children: The Spanish Cross-Sectional InProS Project." *Nutrients* 11, no. 5 (May 2, 2019): 1,007. https://doi.org/10.3390/nu11051007.

Katsagoni, Christina N. Glykeria Psarra, Michael Georgoulis, Konstantinos Tambalis, Demosthenes B. Panagiotakos, and Labros S. Sidossis. "High and Moderate Adherence to Mediterranean Lifestyle Is Inversely Associated with Overweight, General and Abdominal Obesity in Children and Adolescents: The MediLIFE-Index." *Nutrition Research* 73 (January 2020): 38–47. https://doi.org/10.1016/j.nutres.2019.09.009.

Ferrer-Cascales, Rosario, Natalia Albaladejo-Blázquez, Nicolás Ruiz-Robledillo, Violeta Clement-Carbonell, Miriam Sánchez-SanSegundo, and Ana Zaragoza-Martí. "Higher Adherence to the Mediterranean Diet Is Related to More Subjective Happiness in Adolescents: The Role of Health-Related Quality of Life." *Nutrients* 11, no. 3 (March 25, 2019): 698. https://doi.org/10.3390/nu11030698.

Phytochemicals

Leri, M., M. Scuto, M.L. Ontario, V. Calabrese, E.J. Calabrese, M. Bucciantini, and M. Stefani. "Healthy Effects of Plant Polyphenols: Molecular Mechanisms." *International Journal of Molecular Sciences* 21, no. 4 (2020): 1250. https://doi.org/10.3390/ijms21041250.

Ahmed, S.M.U., L. Luo, A. Namani, X.J. Wang, and X. Tang. "Nrf2 Signaling Pathway: Pivotal Roles in Inflammation." *Biochimica et Biophysica Acta (BBA)—Molecular Basis of Disease* 1863, no. 2 (2017): 585–597. https://doi.org/10.1016/j.bbadis.2016.11.005.

The Evidence Against Food Additives

Trasande, Leonardo, Rachel M. Shaffer, Sheela Sathyanarayana, and Council on Environmental Health. "Food Additives and Child Health." *Pediatrics* 142, no. 2 (August 2018): e20181408. https://doi.org/10.1542/peds.2018-1408.

Additives

Martino, John Vincent, Johan Van Limbergen, and Leah E. Cahill. "The Role of Carrageenan and Carboxymethylcellulose in the Development of Intestinal Inflammation." *Frontiers in Pediatrics* 5 (May 1, 2017). https://doi.org/10.3389/fped.2017.00096.

Sugars

Fidler Mis, N., C. Braegger, J. Bronsky, C. Campoy, M. Domellöf, N.D. Embleton, I. Hojsak, J. Hulst, F. Indrio, A. Lapillonne, W. Mihatsch, C. Molgaard, R. Vora, and M. Fewtrell. "Sugar in Infants, Children and Adolescents: A Position Paper of the European Society for Paediatric Gastroenterology, Hepatology and Nutrition Committee on Nutrition." *Journal of Pediatric Gastroenterology and Nutrition* 65, no. 6 (2017): 681–696. https://doi.org/10.1097/MPG.0000000000001733.

Kessler, D. A. (2009). *The End of Overeating: Taking Control of the Insatiable American Appetite.* Rodale: Distributed to the trade by Macmillan.

Artificial Sugars

Choudhary, Arbind Kumar, and Yeong Yeh Lee. "Neurophysiological Symptoms and Aspartame: What Is the Connection?" *Nutritional Neuroscience* 21, no. 5 (May 28, 2018): 306–16. https://doi.org/10.1080/1028415X.2017.1288340.

Wang, Qiao-Ping, Duncan Browman, Herbert Herzog, and G. Gregory Neely. "Non-Nutritive Sweeteners Possess a Bacteriostatic Effect and Alter Gut Microbiota in Mice." Edited by Marie-Joelle Virolle. *PLOS ONE* 13, no. 7 (July 5, 2018): e0199080. https://doi.org/10.1371/journal.pone.0199080.

Organic

Council on Environmental Health. "Pesticide Exposure in Children." *Pediatrics* 130, no. 6 (2012): e1757–e1763. https://doi.org/10.1542/peds.2012-2757.

Lu, C., D.B. Barr, M.A. Pearson and L.A. Waller. "Dietary Intake and Its Contribution to Longitudinal Organophosphorus Pesticide Exposure in Urban/Suburban Children." *Environmental Health Perspectives* 116, no. 4 (2008): 537–542. https://doi.org/10.1289/ehp.10912.

Lu, C., K. Toepel, R. Irish, R.A. Fenske, D.B. Barr, and R. Bravo. "Organic Diets Significantly Lower Children's Dietary Exposure to Organophosphorus Pesticides." *Environmental Health Perspectives* 114, no. 2 (2006): 260–263. https://doi.org/10.1289/ehp.8418.

Healthy Fats

Gorzynik-Debicka, M., P. Przychodzen, F. Cappello, A. Kuban-Jankowska, A. Marino Gammazza, N. Knap, M. Wozniak, and M. Gorska-Ponikowska. "Potential Health Benefits of Olive Oil and Plant Polyphenols." *International Journal of Molecular Sciences* 19, no. 3 (2018): 686. https://doi.org/10.3390/ijms19030686.

The Anti-Inflammatory Way and the Microbiome

Rinninella, Cintoni, Raoul, Lopetuso, Scaldaferri, Pulcini, Miggiano, Gasbarrini, & Mele. "Food Components and Dietary Habits: Keys for a Healthy Gut Microbiota Composition." *Nutrients* 11, no. 10 (2019): 2,393. https://doi.org/10.3390/nu11102393.

CHAPTER 2
Climate Change

Environmental Working Group, Climate and Environmental Impacts, https://www.ewg.org/meateatersguide/a-meat-eaters-guide-to-climate-change-health-what-you-eat-matters/climate-and-environmental-impacts/.

CHAPTER 3
The Biology of Taste

Bolles, Robert C., ed. *The Hedonics of Taste*. Hillsdale, NJ: L. Erlbaum Associates, 1991.

Mennella, Julie A. "Ontogeny of Taste Preferences: Basic Biology and Implications for Health." *The American Journal of Clinical Nutrition* 99, no. 3 (March 1, 2014): 704S-711S. https://doi.org/10.3945/ajcn.113.067694.

Taste Development in Pregnancy and Infancy

Beauchamp, Gary K., and Julie A. Mennella. "Flavor Perception in Human Infants: Development and Functional Significance." *Digestion* 83, no. 1 (2011): 1–6. https://doi.org/10.1159/000323397.

Nicklaus, Sophie. "The Role of Food Experiences during Early Childhood in Food Pleasure Learning." *Appetite* 104 (September 2016): 3–9. https://doi.org/10.1016/j.appet.2015.08.022.

Introducing Solid Foods

Schwartz, C., P.A.M.J. Scholtens, A. Lalanne, H. Weenen, and S. Nicklaus. "Development of Healthy Eating Habits Early in Life. Review of Recent Evidence and Selected Guidelines." *Appetite* 57, no. 3 (2011): 796–807. https://doi.org/10.1016/j.appet.2011.05.316.

Caton, S.J., P. Blundell, S.M. Ahern, C. Nekitsing, A. Olsen, P. Møller, H. Hausner, E. Remy, S. Nicklaus, C. Chabanet, S. Issanchou, and M.M. Hetherington. "Learning to Eat Vegetables in Early Life: The Role of Timing, Age and Individual Eating Traits." *PLoS ONE* 9, no. 5 (2014): e97609. https://doi.org/10.1371/journal.pone.0097609.

Barends, Coraline, Jeanne H.M. de Vries, Jos Mojet, and Cees de Graaf. "Effects of Starting Weaning Exclusively with Vegetables on Vegetable Intake at the Age of 12 and 23 Months." *Appetite* 81 (October 2014): 193–99. https://doi.org/10.1016/j.appet.2014.06.023.

Northstone, K., P. Emmett, F. Nethersole, and the ALSPAC Study Team. "The Effect of Age of Introduction to Lumpy Solids on Foods Eaten and Reported Feeding Difficulties at 6 and 15 Months." *Journal of Human Nutrition and Dietetics* 14, no. 1 (February 2001): 43–54. https://doi.org/10.1046/j.1365-277X.2001.00264.x.

School-Age Kids

Anzman-Frasca, Stephanie, and Sarah Ehrenberg. "Learning to Like: Roles of Repeated Exposure and Other Types of Learning." In *Pediatric Food Preferences and Eating Behaviors*, by Julie C Lumeng and Jennifer O Fisher, 2018. http://proxy.uqtr.ca/login.cgi?action=login&u=uqtr&db=sciencedir&ezurl=http://www.sciencedirect.com/science/book/9780128117163.

Nicklaus, Sophie. "Complementary Feeding Strategies to Facilitate Acceptance of Fruits and Vegetables: A Narrative Review of the Literature." *International Journal of Environmental Research and Public Health* 13, no. 11 (November 19, 2016): 1,160. https://doi.org/10.3390/ijerph13111160.

Teens

Forestell, Catherine A. "The Development of Flavor Perception and Acceptance: The Roles of Nature and Nurture." In *Nestlé Nutrition Institute Workshop Series*, edited by M.S. Fewtrell, F. Haschke, and S.L. Prescott, 85:135–43. S. Karger AG, 2016. https://doi.org/10.1159/000439504.

Mitigating Allergies through Early Exposure

Kusari, Ayan, Allison Han, and Lawrence Eichenfield. "Recent Advances in Understanding and Preventing Peanut and Tree Nut Hypersensitivity." *F1000Research* 7 (October 30, 2018): 1,716. https://doi.org/10.12688/f1000research.14450.1.

Szajewska, Hania, Raanan Shamir, Luisa Mearin, Carmen Ribes-Koninckx, Carlo Catassi, Magnus Domellöf, Mary S. Fewtrell, et al. "Gluten Introduction and the Risk of Coeliac Disease: A Position Paper by the European Society for Pediatric Gastroenterology, Hepatology, and Nutrition." *Journal of Pediatric Gastroenterology and Nutrition* 62, no. 3 (March 2016): 507–13. https://doi.org/10.1097/MPG.0000000000001105.

Du Toit, G., G. Roberts, P.H. Sayre, H.T. Bahnson, S. Radulovic, A.F. Santos, H.A. Brough, D. Phippard, M. Basting, M. Feeney, V. Turcanu, M.L. Sever,

M. Gomez Lorenzo, M. Plaut, and G. Lack. Sever, M. L., Gomez Lorenzo, M., Plaut, M., & Lack, G. (2015). "Randomized Trial of Peanut Consumption in Infants at Risk for Peanut Allergy." *New England Journal of Medicine* 372, no. 9 (2015): 803–813. https://doi.org/10.1056/NEJMoa1414850.

Du Toit, George, Graham Roberts, Peter H. Sayre, Marshall Plaut, Henry T. Bahnson, Herman Mitchell, Suzana Radulovic, et al. "Identifying Infants at High Risk of Peanut Allergy: The Learning Early About Peanut Allergy (LEAP) Screening Study." *Journal of Allergy and Clinical Immunology* 131, no. 1 (January 2013): 135-143.e12. https://doi.org/10.1016/j.jaci.2012.09.015.

Perkin, Michael R., Kirsty Logan, Anna Tseng, Bunmi Raji, Salma Ayis, Janet Peacock, Helen Brough, et al. "Randomized Trial of Introduction of Allergenic Foods in Breast-Fed Infants." *New England Journal of Medicine* 374, no. 18 (May 5, 2016): 1,733–43. https://doi.org/10.1056/NEJMoa1514210.

Modeling Healthy and Adventurous Eating

Bauer, Anna, Florencia Jesús, María José Gómez Ramos, Ana Lozano, and Amadeo Rodríguez Fernández-Alba. "Identification of Unexpected Chemical Contaminants in Baby Food Coming from Plastic Packaging Migration by High Resolution Accurate Mass Spectrometry." *Food Chemistry* 295 (October 2019): 274–88. https://doi.org/10.1016/j.foodchem.2019.05.105.

Emmett, P. M., N.P. Hays, and C.M. Taylor. "Antecedents of Picky Eating Behaviour in Young Children." *Appetite* 130:163–173. https://doi.org/10.1016/j.appet.2018.07.032.

CHAPTER 4
Eat Together As a Family

Fiese, Barbara H., and Marlene Schwartz. "Reclaiming the Family Table: Mealtimes and Child Health and Wellbeing." Society for Research in Child Development, 2008. https://files.eric.ed.gov/fulltext/ED521697.pdf.

Encourage Mindful (and Screen-Free!) Eating

Warren, Janet M., Nicola Smith, and Margaret Ashwell. "A Structured Literature Review on the Role of Mindfulness, Mindful Eating and Intuitive Eating in Changing Eating Behaviours: Effectiveness and Associated Potential Mechanisms." *Nutrition Research Reviews* 30, no. 2 (December 2017): 272–83. https://doi.org/10.1017/S0954422417000154.

Make the Healthy Choice the Easy Choice

Elliott, Charlene, and Emily Truman. "Measuring the Power of Food Marketing to Children: A Review of Recent Literature." *Current Nutrition Reports*, November 14, 2019. https://doi.org/10.1007/s13668-019-00292-2.

Henry, Holly K. M., and Dina L. G. Borzekowski. "The Nag Factor: A Mixed-Methodology Study in the US of Young Children's Requests for Advertised Products." *Journal of Children and Media* 5, no. 3 (August 2011): 298–317. https://doi.org/10.1080/17482798.2011.584380.

Ensaff, Hannah, Matt Homer, Pinki Sahota, Debbie Braybrook, Susan Coan, and Helen McLeod. "Food Choice Architecture: An Intervention in a Secondary School and Its Impact on Students' Plant-Based Food Choices." *Nutrients* 7, no. 6 (June 2, 2015): 4,426–37. https://doi.org/10.3390/nu7064426.

Limit Snacking

Piernas, Carmen, and Barry M. Popkin. "Trends in Snacking among U.S. Children." *Health Affairs* 29, no. 3 (March 2010): 398–404. https://doi.org/10.1377/hlthaff.2009.0666.

Cook Together!

Ehrenberg, S., L.A. Leone, B. Sharpe, K. Reardon, and S. Anzman-Frasca. "Using Repeated Exposure through Hands-on Cooking to Increase Children's Preferences for Fruits and Vegetables." *Appetite* 142 (November 2019): 104347. https://doi.org/10.1016/j.appet.2019.104,347.

Acknowledgments

Thanks to our nutrition advisors:

Amy Dean, MPH, RD, LDN, Children's Hospital of Philadelphia

Maria Hanna, MS, RD, LDN, Children's Hospital of Philadelphia

We are grateful to Amy Dean and Maria Hanna, both experienced pediatric registered dietitian nutritionists, who encouraged this book and provided practice-based content ideas. A special thanks to Amy, who helped make sure that the content and recipes were applicable and adaptable for children and families.

Thanks to Chetana Divya Lagisetti for her thorough (and speedy!) work researching phytochemicals. Thanks to Ellen Barker, Anastasia Wilkerson, Naxielly Dominguez, and everyone at Children's Aid Society's food and nutrition program for their work, which helped lay the foundation for many recipes and activities in this book (and to Naxielly for her brilliant Banana Quinoa Muffins). Thanks Molly Weingrod and family for the Sweet Potato Silver Dollars.

The Drexel Food Lab provided recipe testing for all of the recipes in this book.

Special thanks to Natalie Shaak for her editing superpowers, Chef Rachel Sherman for her leadership, and all of the students including Kwame Amuh, Carrie Bonnell, Katelyn Comerford, Antoinette Hicks, Laura King, Rosa Morar, Erik Ildefonzo, Lauren Miller, Olivia Spratt, Catriona Andress, Nora Vaughan, and Anna Wilson. Special thanks to Chef Rich Pepino and Dr. Rosemary Trout of the Department of Food and Hospitality Management at Drexel University.

Thanks to Max Sinsheimer for believing in this project and Jacqueline Musser and her team at Simon & Schuster for nurturing it.

Thanks to the patients of Drs. Mascarenhas and McClafferty and their families. Thanks also to our colleagues, teachers, and mentors at all institutions who have guided and shaped this work.

Special thanks are due to our families who have endured plenty of recipe testing outtakes, evening and weekend conference calls, and late nights writing. Your support is everything.

Index

About the Authors

Stefania Patinella is the founder of Seed to Table, where she provides integrative wellness coaching to families grappling with chronic health conditions at the intersection of the gastrointestinal, nervous, and immune systems. She has seventeen years' experience teaching nutrition and healthful cooking to diverse audiences, from children and families to healthcare professionals. Previously, she was founding director of the Go!Healthy cooking, nutrition education, and gardening programs at the Children's Aid Society, a nonprofit serving 70,000 children and families each year in New York City. There she also developed a model meal program for children, replacing all processed foods with whole-foods and plant-based recipes cooked from scratch. She also served as executive director of Healing Kitchens Institute and executive chef at Amherst College. Stefania received her BA from the University of Pennsylvania and MA in health arts and sciences from Goddard College. She also completed her chef's training at the Natural Gourmet Institute and studied herbalism at the Vermont Center for Integrative Herbalism. Mostly, though, she's a humble lover of plants.

Alexandra Romey is the culinary developer at Saxbys, a coffee café with twenty-five locations in and around Philadelphia. She is a graduate of the Culinary Arts program at Drexel University, where she assisted in the founding of the Food Lab. She filed her first patent for a gluten-free baking technology and has published more than one hundred recipes. Alexandra has been recognized by *Foodservice Director* magazine, has received the *Edible Philly*'s Local Hero Award, and was named one of Billy Penn's Young Chefs to Watch in 2017. She has recently completed her masters of education in creativity and innovation at Drexel University.

Hilary McClafferty, MD, FAAP, is board-certified in pediatrics, pediatric emergency medicine, and integrative medicine. She serves as medical director, Pediatric Emergency Medicine, at the

Tucson Medical Center in Arizona. Dr. McClafferty is the founding director of the Pediatric Integrative Medicine in Residency program at the University of Arizona, and past chair of the American Academy of Pediatrics Section on Integrative Medicine. She is chair of the Special Interest Group for Physician Health and Wellness in the Academy, and a founding member of the American Board of Integrative Medicine. She is founder and chief executive officer of the Academy of Pediatric Integrative Medicine. Dr. McClafferty received her medical degree from the University of Michigan and completed pediatric residency training at Northwestern Children's Memorial Hospital in Chicago, and at the University of Arizona in Tucson. She is fellowship-trained in pediatric emergency medicine and certified in clinical hypnosis and trained in medical acupuncture. Dr. McClafferty has authored two textbooks: *Integrative Pediatrics: Art, Science, and Clinical Application*, and *Mind-Body Medicine in Clinical Practice*, both published by Routledge.

Jonathan Deutsch, PhD, is a professor in the Department of Food and Hospitality Management and Department of Nutrition Sciences (courtesy) at Drexel University. Deutsch is director of the Drexel Food Lab, a culinary innovation and food product research and development lab focused on solving real-world food system problems in the areas of sustainability, health promotion, and inclusive dining. He is the author or editor of eight books including *Barbecue: A Global History* (with Megan Elias), *Culinary Improvisation*, and *Gastropolis: Food and Culture in New York City* (with Annie Hauck-Lawson). Deutsch has also authored numerous articles in journals of food studies, public health, and hospitality education. He earned his PhD in food studies and food management from New York University, his culinary degree from The Culinary Institute of America, and is an alumnus of Drexel University.

Maria R. Mascarenhas, MBBS, is a pediatric gastroenterologist in the Division of Gastroenterology, Hepatology, and Nutrition at Children's Hospital of Philadelphia, considered the leading pediatric hospital in the United States. She serves as the director of the Nutrition Support Service, section chief of nutrition in the Division of Gastroenterology and Nutrition, medical director of the Clinical Nutrition Department, medical director of the Healthy Weight Program, and director of the Integrative Health Program. Dr. Mascarenhas received her medical degree from St. John's Medical College in India and her pediatric training at SUNY Downstate Medical Center in Brooklyn and Texas Children's Hospital in Houston. She is board-certified and fellowship-trained in pediatrics, nutrition, and pediatric gastroenterology and certified in clinical hypnosis. She is a professor of pediatrics at the Perelman School of Medicine at the University of Pennsylvania. Dr. Mascarenhas is an international speaker and is widely published.